Survive, Revive, and Thrive

A Guide to Saving Yourself

Claire Frances Moore

CF MOORE

PUBLISHING

Paperback ISBN: 979-8-9905957-0-5

Digital ISBN: 979-8-9905957-1-2

Hardcover ISBN: 979-8-9905957-2-9

LOC Number: 2024908742

Contents

Part Three
Thrive

To my Soul Phamily:

Thank you for your endless love, support, and patience.

All my gratitude,
-C

Introduction

My name is Claire, and I'm just another player in this game we call life. This round, I'm an American female, currently living through the chit-chow that is the twenty-first century. If you're wondering if these are typos, they're not; we'll get to the "ch" thing later.

I have a Master of Science in chemical engineering and work full-time in the corporate food and beverage industry, so it's safe to say I know a thing or two about how the world operates. I went from being trapped in the vicious cycle of working full-time and being gravely underpaid for my talents (only for my paycheck to be consumed by my student loans, avocado toast, overpriced coffee, and other "millennial" demands) to liberating myself to my soul's calling. I went from being plagued with debt, enduring mental health challenges, and possessing the insatiable desire to save the planet, yet feeling powerless to take action, to overcoming my suppressed issues and thriving in life.

Other parts of my journey that I hope you can relate to and find helpful, which will be covered here, include:

- How to lose a hundred pounds ... and what to do if you gain it all back,
- Chemical engineering,
- Drugs (everything from ADHD meds to heroin), and
- How to save the world—because we need your help.

Although it may feel like life is all turmoil, it really is a marvelous time to be alive! If you can put down your dumbphones and ignore the news long enough, you will begin to realize an extraordinary time is unfolding upon us. We are entering a new era where people are collectively awakening and regaining their strength.

Please be aware there are triggering themes here, including emotional abuse, eating disorders, mental illness, medication, drug and alcohol abuse, grief/loss, and veganism. So, buckle up and balance your chakras because we're overcoming past traumas, taking care of ourselves, and moving past this dark period in history. We are currently plagued with great sickness and must heal ourselves individually to heal ourselves collectively. We are one.

I'm here to awaken you to the fact you hold great power on an individual level, even though so many of us are unconsciously giving it away. I want you to learn to take that power back. We must give ourselves more credit for the work we are doing and not succumb to the victim mentality. Life rewards you when you show up.

This writing is for anyone who has had the courage to be vulnerable enough to put their heart and soul into their work, while simultaneously finding and making themselves whole in the process. As I share my story with you, I encourage you to share yours with the world. You never know who you may save by telling your story.

From my whole heart,

—Claire

Part One
Survive

Chapter 1: And We Healed

There I was, suffering from chronic corporate burnout, working ten-plus hours a day on my feet, supporting a team of ten-plus product development scientists who all needed me at the same time. I would hide at my desk just to sit down for a minute and often skipped lunch because it was easier to power through it. I couldn't afford an hour break in the middle of the day. They needed me, so I felt bad.

After twisting my ankle (unrelated to work) a few months prior and not seeking proper medical attention, I found it starting to swell up to the size of a baseball by the end of the work week. I took the weekend to recover and rest, sometimes, and then I repeated the cycle and was crying in pain again by the next Friday. I was too afraid to say anything. They needed me. I was irreplaceable. So, this cycle continued, week after week.

I so desperately needed a break—a deep, restful reset. A lovely, month-long nap buried in my bed would suffice instead of crawling to the coffeepot the minute I woke up. *But how will that ever happen? I* thought. *There's no way I can just take a month off like when I was in college.*

Then my prayers were answered. The world shut down. "Thanks, Dr. Fauci," I say with a cringe. We were sent to work from home the day the New York governor mandated the shutdown or else corporate would have kept us there. My goddaughter was born that day—March 18, 2020.

Life didn't change much for me, I'm grateful to say. Except it did.

Quarantining was an introvert's wet dream—hanging out at home with our pets, plans getting canceled, normalizing saying no to social gatherings, binge-watching our comfort shows, no traffic, sleeping in, and resting. Interviews became video chats, removing aspects of social anxiety. You could turn off the webcam whether your boss liked it or not and take many glorious hammock naps in the sunshine.

I was grateful for time to rest and recover, grateful to adapt to these changes, grateful to still have a job, despite growing to despise what I was doing by contributing to the immoral practice of manipulating another species' reproductive system for profit. (We'll get into the specifics shortly.)

The world quieted down. We spent time in our homes and learned how to cook new meals. We completed house projects and contributed to that dreadful line at Home Depot. Nurses finally got the recognition they deserve.

Many people were demanding salons and restaurants open back up—I hope you remember that next time you leave a bad tip. So many people were obsessing over *Tiger King*, blinded to the fact it was based on breeding and exploiting wild animals. People died from drug overdoses. Some of my friends and family died from drug overdoses. There wasn't much for some people to do except sit with themselves and get high to try to escape it.

The Amazon rainforest was burning down so we could farm cattle for cheap hamburgers. Consumers demanded it by purchasing fast food.

The news distracted us with stories of famous people dying and COVID-19. We were (and still are) so desperate for a leader that we blindly followed the news, showing us how divided we are, how ready everyone is to fight each other, and how ready everyone is to tear each other down. Social media gave people a sense of entitlement to make claims about things they have no actual knowledge of (masks, vaccines, poli-dicks).

Even with the gracious opportunity to sit at home alone, a wave of anxiety still hung over my head; a sense of unease lingered. Working from home, I felt the need to be glued to my work computer. I was nervous I would miss an instant message or an email, and someone would say I wasn't working. It made me want to close the laptop and throw it across the room. I was saying yes when I wanted to say no. I was overextending myself and grew nervous about returning to the office. I started to pick up bad habits like sleeping too much and eating trash.

I missed smiles, live music, and hugs—but the world so deeply needed a reset. It was a chance for everything to quiet down. Even though I was not content, I knew it was a chance to sit with ourselves and dig deep, a chance to ask ourselves, *Why do we feel like this? What is making us this anxious? Where are we hurting?*

Something was still wrong, out of alignment. We were still living in fear. So, we finally sought external help instead of silently battling it internally like every other time. We ended the mental health stigma. We identified the root cause instead of coping. We surrendered and found our medicine.

We asked ourselves, *What are we hiding from? What are we burying? Who hurt us most and why? Where and why are we holding resentment? What are we most afraid of—and why?*

When we are comfortable enough to sit alone with ourselves and ask these questions and are willing to do the work to remediate the destruction, that is when we will thrive.

The pandemic gave us time to find that comfort. We dug deep. We cried hard when we found it. We brought it to the surface to transmute and repair and ensure we never let it happen again.

We danced with our demons and invited them to sit down for tea and cookies. We did some hardcore self-evaluating and confronted what we were so desperately trying to hide from. We identified our triggers—person, place, or thing—and asked ourselves why we operate the way we do.

We left behind destructive habits and unhealthy relationships. We left behind all that does not align with what we are becoming. We took back our energy and poured it into ourselves instead of everyone else and got to know ourselves without outside influence.

We hibernated and healed. We stopped our unhealthy coping mechanisms, like replying to uplifting comments with sarcasm and disbelief, and instead smiled and said, "Thank you." We abolished our fear of failure and went for it anyway. We stood up for ourselves and the ones who came before us who were unable to. We used this time to reflect deeply on ourselves and become different people—for the better, of course.

We broke down our own barriers—the barriers we were holding up against ourselves, holding us back from our authenticity—to find our bliss. We followed our passions, created, and fell in love with life again.

This shutdown of society forced me to confront the emotions and pain I had spent years suppressing. It forced me to voice my opinions and needs. It forced me to take the initiative to step into alignment, to do what I came here to do.

I know you're suffering. I know you want to get better but don't know where to begin. It's not too late. It's never too late. You can do this now. Nobody is going to take care of you like yourself. As soon as you stop seeking external validation and start taking responsibility, it will all start to turn around.

The time has come to get it together. We owe it to ourselves to move past our pain and stop self-sabotaging. Some don't want to change—and won't. There is a true "comfort in being sad," as Kurt Cobain said. Some will live life in the familiarity of their comfort zones even when it's not what they truly desire. They settle because it's easier. You can't change them; you can only change yourself. You're the only one who will always be there for you. Change isn't easy, but the other side is always brighter, and you can get there.

Chapter 2: $C_{21}H_{30}O_5$

I was born on the cusp of Taurus season, the universe deeming me to have an eye for beauty, a taste for pleasure, a thirst for knowledge, and food to be a prevalent theme in my life. I have at least fifty tabs open on my phone and another hundred in my head, and I am always writing something down. I'm here to deliver a dash of cynical realism, sprinkled with intellect, blessed with the divine gift of common sense. I have always been on the run from society's traditions. Never have I ever: used any dating apps, dyed my hair, watched reality TV, done the cinnamon challenge or any Tik Tok dances, the list goes on. There have been times when I have felt like a stranger in my own skin and have had trouble advocating for myself. After enduring a miraculous, yet painful, transformation, I have established a level of self-love that is impervious to penetration. I am here to share my story with you and encourage you to commence your own.

Before all that, though, I was born into a working-class, suburban neighborhood in Westchester, New York, and couldn't be more grateful that my hometown would not be one of the struggles I faced in life. I absolutely loved growing up in New York, where authenticity reigns and our parallel parking skills are superior.

Where I was located (the 914), some people (the 631) would deem upstate, but it's not really upstate for anyone who actually knows New York. My town was only about an hour north of the city, not even close to actual "upstate". It was where you could experience all seasons on the same day in October, and the trees on the side of the highway looked like pieces of moldavite. It was where people were willing to help you with whatever you needed but would curse you out if you made them late for work. I will forever cherish the balance between the fluidity and rigidity of the East Coast, where we adapt to change effortlessly but are always in a rush to the next red light. We thrive in chaos and get stuff done efficiently but will, deadass, get mad scrappy if we have beef with youse.

My mom is from Staten Island, and my dad is from the Bronx, but this isn't about to be the classic New York love story you may be expecting. Mom worked most of the time as a registered nurse in New York City, saving lives. She sacrificed and provided for the family. It amazes me I didn't inherit her work ethic. I loved my mom; she was always my biggest supporter. She was kind and generous and would stop what she was doing to help me with whatever I needed.

Dad, on the other hand, was ill-tempered and unpredictable. He possessed a plethora of knowledge but needed to work on the delivery. He did not read others' emotions well and would just talk someone's ear off and couldn't tell if they retained a word he was saying. He was a leather craftsman who dabbled in his brother's taxidermy business. So, as I was growing up, your stuffed animals and my stuffed animals had different meanings.

I have one younger sister, who is rather unhinged. She should write her own book, but her story, through my eyes, will be told in this one.

Despite having a relatively privileged upbringing, I grew up to be an emotionally dysregulated mess. We always went on vacation and had food on the table, but were taught to neglect our emotions when we were in turmoil. We had new clothes and supplies for school every year, but someone was always so angry and yelling at someone else over minuscule tasks. Dad never ditched the family by going out to get milk and never returning, but was constantly berating everyone about their physical appearance. Cue the start of my mental health deterioration.

My parents were married, but someone was always fighting, and no conversation could take place without someone sounding annoyed or frustrated. Mom was gone a lot, working. I missed her and wished she was home with me. I always felt safer with her around. Dad worked from home and spent his time in the basement or outside doing yard work.

There were no demonstrations of teamwork within my family. When Mom was in emotional distress, Dad belittled it and told her, "It's not that big of a deal" or "It's all in your head." Mom kept the peace, so the fight was not perpetuated. When Dad instilled rage, Mom did anything to try to keep the peace and told us, "Don't let Dad bother you." When I asked my dad for help or advice, it was always "go ask your mother" rarely "let's figure this out together."

This was what I looked up to, growing up. This was what my subconscious deemed as "normal". I used to think that when I found "the one", part of it would be me being comfortable disrespecting and yelling at them. When you grow up around this, you have no idea what a healthy relationship looks like, and you dive, face first, into an unhealthy one because it feels normal.

There was lots of yelling and a lack of love in my house growing up. Dad was going deaf and needed to wear hearing aids but refused. He liked to watch TV, so the volume on that took precedence over what was happening in the living room. After we finally convinced him to get them, insurance didn't want to cover it because my mother made too much money as a nurse working in New York City. After enduring the battles between the insurance company, we finally got him the hearing aids. He didn't wear them. Instead, he listened to classical music so loud I felt like I was in an insane asylum.

Love was transactional in my household; I was only sought out by my dad when I was asked to do something. I was asked to do the dishes before I could even sit down to eat. When I would do them, he would watch me and correct every move I made, making me even more uncomfortable. I was asked to do chores the second I walked through the door before being asked how my day was, or if I was even okay. If I said no, the request would be manipulated into, "Do it for your hardworking mother so she doesn't have to do it when she gets home." And of course, when I asked for something, it turned into a contingency.

I was berated for every move I tried to make by those who wanted to gain a sense of power over me because the love was missing. I couldn't do anything without being yelled at and criticized. Opening a window to get some fresh air wasn't okay because the wood burning stove was on to keep the house warm. I was yelled at for not turning the oil burner off after taking a shower because we had to conserve hot water. I was yelled at for putting the dog's leash on the couch instead of the coat hanger. A mere task such as taking photos became a tense ordeal because I got yelled at for not holding the camera the right way. I was yelled at if I cleaned the cast iron pan with soap, even when I used whatever weird cleaning tool he had for it. I was yelled at if I didn't compost a vegetable scrap. I was yelled at if I left my toothbrush on the sink. I was yelled at if I left my shampoo in the shower. I was yelled at when I left my shoes and backpack in the living room instead of my own. I was yelled at for taking up space.

So, I started to tune out. I wasn't doing anything wrong, and when I was constantly berated about my actions, I chose to ignore it. Now, I wasn't the perfect child. I had no problem doing chores or contributing, but I had a problem when that was the only thing being asked of me. I felt as if I existed for the disposal of tasks. I tried to rebel by not listening, in hopes my dad would stop asking me to do things, but it had quite the opposite effect. He would end up yelling at me or my sister for not listening, not doing chores, or not helping with outside yard work. Yard work will traumatize anybody. On the days where I had to help with yard work outside, I would pretend to be sick that day and not even get out of bed, exhibiting my fight-or-flight response very early in life.

I was flight; my sister was the opposite. Two children can grow up in the same home with the same parents and have a completely different childhood experience. Fire can melt gold yet harden clay; the difference is in what you're made of, not what happened to you.

From early childhood, my sister displayed many peculiar habits like biting people, getting into fights in the locker room in fifth grade, and wearing black Timberlands in the summer. She's slightly inept at executive functioning despite being one of the most caring people you could meet. Maybe it's because she fell on her head when she was three? Maybe it's because she was told who she was from day one and didn't really have a sense of individuality? Maybe it's because she has played violent video games since she was a kid? Or maybe it's because there was no emotional regulation in our household. Probably that one.

I grew up motivated by fear, enduring unrelenting scolding, with a physical altercation from time to time, from those who could not manage their anger and refused to do anything about it. My plan was to gain control of the situation by avoiding them and letting them struggle instead of taking their blatant disrespect, which, of course, only added to the rising tension and continued the vicious cycle.

When I wouldn't listen, he would start yelling, cut the wires to my electronics, or kick my toys around the room, right out of my hands. I would have to duck and cover my head to avoid getting hit with anything or try to run to my room. That didn't work because he would just chase me, and I didn't have a locking door. I would barricade myself on the other side and use all my strength to keep it from slamming open. That was the first time I was ever thankful for being heavy enough to hold the door closed while Mr. Anger Management fiercely tried to bang it down from the other side. It was also my first panic attack. My whole body tensed, I couldn't catch my breath, I was hysterically crying, and I couldn't tell anyone. I was terrified.

Nothing screams childhood trauma like your dad's favorite fictional character being Miss Trunchbull and him wanting to construct his own "Chokey" downstairs to lock you in for not listening. I longed for the day when the hairs on the back of my neck wouldn't stand up when I heard footsteps coming up the stairs. I grew up afraid of him. I was not able to look him in the eye and wanted to run away when I was in the same room as him. But that's your family, so you give them chance after chance.

Growing up surrounded by ceaseless hostility with people who were so comfortable with discomfort, I was turned off from my parents' behavior. Home isn't supposed to be where the idea of love is your dad punching you in the arm and mocking you when you say, "Don't touch me." Their touch lingers on your skin and hurts long after their hands are off you.

My own home quickly began to feel like a foreign prison, and I would often retreat to my room. I was only sought out when the dishwasher needed to be emptied, the table needed to be set, the floor needed to be swept, or some other minor chore needed to be completed.

When I sat down to dinner, I would get scolded by my father to "take human bites" while trying to eat. (How the fug else are you supposed to eat sushi?) It made me instantly lose my appetite and retreat into solitude and cry. It made me so angry, and I grew uncomfortable to take a bite of food in front of anyone.

I couldn't bring myself to go into the kitchen to eat if there was anyone else in there, so I would sneak into the kitchen when it was empty and uncontrollably binge on junk food until I heard footsteps coming up the stairs. I would drop whatever I was doing and run to my room and close the door.

When I started to gain weight from binge-eating, there were constant shots taken at my appearance, all coming from those closest who were supposed to protect me. As a helpless child, who could not fend for themselves, all I needed at the time was to be protected and loved, but I received quite the opposite. My environment didn't protect me, so binge-eating did. In some weird way, it was my body's way of making me feel safe and allowing me to cope emotionally.

I was overweight and uncomfortable in my own skin for as long as I could remember. From a very young age, I learned to punish and shame my body and tied my self-worth to the number on the scale. Outside comments and growing up in diet culture increased my discomfort exponentially.

Outside influence constantly commenting on your weight will really fug you up. You'll grow up with a sense of self-hatred and body dysmorphia. You have the idea ingrained in your head that nobody will find you attractive. You start forming strong detachments from yourself and from those who made the comments and feel bad because they're your family.

I was living in constant dismay, walking on eggshells. Everyone in my family was clearly suffering but unable to voice it—avoiding their emotions and pretending it was all good all the time, so focused on working they neglected to see that one daughter was depressed and the other was using hard drugs. We'll get into that later.

We called a family meeting to try to relieve some of the tension because nobody knew how to effectively, calmly communicate with each other. When asked what was bothering me, I choked up and cried.

I tried to voice what was bothering me, but all I could muster was how he didn't care about anything except me doing chores—nothing about the lack of support for my emotional well-being. I didn't even know what I needed at the time, but I knew it wasn't this. Growing up in an Irish Catholic household, all of my problems were deemed "not that bad" or they would "give me something to worry about". The guilt of having emotions was prominent.

My emotional turmoil was brushed off as overreacting, so I suffered in silence because I felt as though I couldn't safely express my emotions. I was told everything was okay and to "just relax" when I was angry or upset. Showing emotions was not welcomed because no one knew how to deal with them.

Emotional absence from your parents will really fug you up. You'll have no idea how to deal with your emotions and feel bad displaying them in front of people because you'll feel like a burden. You don't want to bother anyone, so you just cry, alone, in your closet. You don't want to complain because you're not actively doing anything to alleviate your harmful situation. Being perpetually exposed to stressful situations I couldn't handle at that age led me to just shut down to avoid the things I couldn't handle.

Despite growing up with fear and rage instilled in me, I did not turn into an angry person. I always had the desire to be the complete opposite. However, I adopted other habits as normal, which were clearly not: ignoring my intuition, allowing myself to be disrespected, not saying what was on my mind for the sake of keeping the peace. These all led me to make some questionable and rash decisions in adulthood while accepting unacceptable behavior from others.

By the grace of the divine, I was gifted with intelligence and common sense. I was smart and excelled in school. I was proficient in math and chemistry and loved music, so that's where I put my focus. I tuned out most of high school with headphones in my ears but still got by because the curriculum caters to those with a photographic memory.

Except, I didn't avoid chemistry class. It was the only class I cared about, and my chemistry teacher could be scary and kick you out of class if you didn't do your work. She kept a stuffed deer leg in her drawer, and she would threaten to hit you with it if you didn't pay attention or failed a test. Learning instilled by fear was a common theme in my childhood.

I was made fun of in school by people who were crawling with their own insecurities. It's a lot more avoidable if you're nice to people, but then you're nice to people for the sake of trying not to get made fun of and turn into a people-pleaser with no boundaries to protect yourself. People in grade school are brutal. They instill their own trauma in others. It's unavoidable. I know people who have gotten divorced before twenty-four, and they still say it wasn't as bad as grade school, where you met the "friends" who stabbed you in the back and taught you your first real lesson in heartbreak.

My self-hatred became much more prominent after having to hang on the pull-up bar in front of the whole gym class for the physical fitness test. I wouldn't change in the locker room and pretended to be sick when it was time to run the mile. I pretended to be sick the day we did the physics experiment where we had to weigh ourselves to calculate the amount of horsepower we produced running up the steps. I pretended to have an injury the day we had to take the physical fitness tests in gym. I soon began making up any excuse whenever I had to do anything remotely uncomfortable. And let me tell you, all that hurts a whole lot worse than getting hit in the face with that red rubber kickball.

So, what happens when you are ashamed of yourself? Whether it be from outside conditioning or self-destruction, you compartmentalize and bury the pieces of yourself you're ashamed of. You try to put on a facade and make yourself look like someone you're not through actions like wearing oversized clothes, people-pleasing, and skipping meals—only to binge on fast food later and hate yourself even more. I was too uncomfortable to even care if I was gaining more weight. My body grew tense and rigid, and I couldn't open up to anybody, including myself.

Then I would go back home to my tense household. I rarely wanted to go home after school, but I put on a mask in front of my family and pretended everything was okay.

I told myself I was hungry and went into the kitchen to binge on processed garbage. I was out of tune with my body and was unable to distinguish between hunger and emotions and used food as an emotional crutch. I was out of control around food and could not regulate my eating habits. I didn't know the impact my food choices would have on me. I was a kid; I didn't do the food shopping. I would eat whatever was in the kitchen, and to excess: a bag of cheese covered popcorn, a bag tortilla chips with melted American cheese, a sleeve of cookies, cups of sugary cereals, handfuls of preserved frozen foods, a bag of pretzels with a packet cream cheese, you name it. No wonder I was overweight and had a face full of acne going into high school. I felt like a stranger in my own body.

So, what do you do when home isn't a safe space and school isn't a safe space? You dissociate to a safe space in your head. Just like training your brain to see the positive in every situation, you can train your brain to dissociate in stressful situations. This led me down the path of dissociation with a bunch of unhealthy coping mechanisms. I used to daydream that I was Princess Mia, imagining some long-lost grandma would come along and tell me I was born into royalty or daydream I would marry into it. I was longing to go home but didn't know where that was because it sure wasn't where I was.

Welcome to survival mode.

For those who cannot empathize with this type of pain, know this: it's more than your parents were mean to you. Perpetual feelings of unsafety shift your nervous system into a chronic state of fight-or-flight mode. When it happens at such a young age, one's brain does not have the chance to develop properly because it's focused on survival. This is how disorders like CPTSD and ADHD can manifest.

Undiagnosed mental illness peppered on top of everything prevented me from functioning correctly, which led to incessant scolding for not functioning correctly. When I couldn't follow directions, I was scolded. When I didn't listen, I was scolded. When I did something wrong, I was scolded. Instead of trying to remediate the situation and get to the root cause of why this was happening, the most they did was buy a book called *How to Talk So Kids Will Listen and Listen So Kids Will Talk*, but it just sat on the shelf, unread. Everything continued as "normal".

Not getting your emotional needs met in childhood will have you growing up to either exclude the ones who hurt you or become hypervigilant of their next move. You abandon your nervous system and become empathetic to those around you. Events from childhood, no matter how insignificant they may seem at the time, stick with you throughout your entire life.

How do we cope? We find things that make us feel good outside of external influence or opinion.

I found my solace in music. It took me away from my harsh reality and partially rejuvenated the depleted serotonin in my brain. Music was always there for whatever mood I was experiencing. I even returned a pair of Tiffany earrings so I could get a guitar instead for my sweet sixteen. Obviously, I got into the punk, emo, depressed teenager, punch-a-hole-in-the-wall music scene. My favorites were Fall Out Boy, Alkaline Trio, and All Time Low. And Nirvana—I fell in love with Nirvana. They put words to my anger and distress because I was unable to. Their lyrics were beautiful melodies that spoke to my soul. Certain songs found me in divine timing (receiving the things we are a vibrational match to at the time we need them). Their lyrics gave me hope when I had nothing else to look forward to.

I made two best friends who liked the same music and loathed high school as much as I did. What better way to bond? We started going to a bunch of concerts to keep ourselves occupied. There was always at least one on the calendar to look forward to. They were the only thing I looked forward to besides graduating high school and never having to set foot in that place again.

Live music was the fuel to my fire; nothing quite lit up my world like that. Live music brings people with shared interests together. Everyone's there for the same purpose, thousands of people singing the same words straight from their soul. It's the only crowd where I didn't feel lonely. Plus, body-slamming people in mosh pits helped me release my anger and rage. There's a reason we feel good when we're dancing to live music and bad when we're stuck inside all day, working when it's sunny out. Music is basically a drug, but one that you can put on repeat and listen to over and over again without it destroying your entire life.

Music always caught and held me when the world was scary. For me, everything was scary all the time, so all I did was listen to music—

all throughout school, when I got home until I went to sleep. I had a hard time paying attention in school and was yet to be diagnosed with ADHD, so I just zoned out and listened to music. My attention flew straight out the window and danced with my daydreams. I am grateful for my photographic memory because that was how I survived high school. I grew my hair so long no one could tell I had headphones in all day, the kind that still had the wires on them.

So, there I was, at high school graduation, weighing my heaviest and afraid to sit down on the flimsy chair for fear of breaking it. That was one of my worst fears at the time—breaking something I sat on in public. I didn't think I would be able to take the humiliation. I had headphones in my ears and my iPod tucked into my bra. I was a master of hiding it at this point. I wanted so desperately to change, but I felt so stagnant. I couldn't wait to get out of there.

Cue college.

Chapter 3: Fear and Loathing in Times Square

I flew away from the nest, about an hour south right into the middle of New York City. It was such a different world than what I grew up in. As much as I loved my private backyard and all the trees, I quickly fell in love with the organized chaos of NYC.

The authenticity of New York is unmatched. It's the only place where you can sing along to Biggie Smalls in a bar at four AM then go next door and eat pizza for one dollar. You meet the special kind of people who can walk down the street while eating, drinking, smoking, talking on the phone, and hailing a cab, who will curse you out if you're a slow walker. New York breeds us tough and unbreakable on the outside, but we are passionate lovers at our core. We are the beautiful balance of an antisocial extrovert and social introvert.

Many despise the city, but there are worse things to consume than fried city street rats from the food trucks and getting pooped on by pigeons in Central Park can't be the worst thing that could happen. Sure, it smells like piss and garbage, but there's nothing like partying on a rooftop all night, then getting to watch the sunrise over the skyline. The magical hue of the NYC skyline makes you feel as if you are living in a dream.

There's stuff that's considered normal in NYC that the rest of the world raises their eyebrows at: being surrounded by water, yet unable to swim in it, or paying sky high rent for a closet-sized room and witnessing your neighbor's morning glories whether you want to or not. "Move to the fifth floor," they said. "It will be fun," they said. We had to leave furniture on the rooftop when the lease ended because there was no elevator, and it was easier than moving it down the stairs.

It's normal for people to be jackhammering the sidewalk outside of the window at seven in the morning on the weekend. It's normal to see people dressed up on the street as Minnie Mouse or Spiderman, demanding money when you ask to take a picture with them. And if you don't pay them, they'll chase you down the street.

You can find billionaires in luxury penthouses while homeless people beg for change on the street in front of the building. Everyone has a drawer full of little sauce packets and plastic utensils they will never use. And where else can you buy a sandwich, more beer, cigarettes, and occasionally, party favors at four AM besides a bodega?

No New Yorker would ever make those poor horses carry us around in carriages, we'll leave that to the clueless tourists. We would never set foot on a tour bus, and we avoid Times Square at all costs. We would never go to the ball drop on New Year's Eve—the savvy ones know the real party is at Madison Square Garden.

The subway is probably the quickest and cheapest way to get around the city, but it's a scary place. There are people who feel obliged to sing loudly and badly, then have the audacity to ask you for a tip. There are rats the size of small cats running around. People have normalized pole dancing and come too close for comfort. You have to avoid eye contact with the homeless people like the plague, or they will try to talk to you. But at least we've built herd immunity after riding the subway.

Everything is so expensive, yet we are so frivolous with our money. We would rather pay a four-dollar ATM fee before walking two blocks to the bank. We're totally comfortable spending sixteen bucks on a gin and tonic (during happy hour) and however much money on drugs after drinking too much. We have debated jaywalking into traffic to open a lawsuit to get someone to pay our student loans. We will spend fifty dollars on a cab to get home because the subways are scary. At least dollar pizza will always be dollar pizza.

If you can drive in the city, you can drive anywhere. We learned how to drive in the harshest conditions and have road rage like no other. We feel the need to lay on the horn 0.01 seconds after the light turns green, but our patience grows even thinner when it comes to the cyclists. It's tight in the city, and everyone's double parked, so if you must drive on the curb to avoid hitting something, it's okay. Yes, we will parallel park your car for you—and tuck that side mirror in.

Living in NYC sparked my creativity. You have to get creative with such a small space. My roommates and I turned the living room into a third bedroom and made our own parking spots by putting traffic cones over fire hydrants so we wouldn't get tickets.

It may be overpopulated, but there are many forward thinkers here. It's a melting pot for ideas and evolution. We learn and adapt to new ways with ease. We are able to carry on a conversation with anyone about anything, using our own, made-up lingo.

- "How ya doin?"
- "It's mad brick out."
- "Deadass."
- "You good?" (and having it mean ten different things)
- "BECSPK."

I appreciated everything NYC had to offer. It was so culturally, economically, and socially diverse. There were endless networking connections. Some of the street art was superb. There was always something to do—live music, Broadway, bars, free yoga, Pickle Day on the Lower East Side. You can find authentic cuisine from any ethnicity. And of course, the bodegas: open twenty-four hours, and ruled by bodega cats that sell single cigarettes for a dollar. It's technically illegal, but you can easily find the spots that still do it. My favorite was the ability to see any concert I wanted. No venues had compared to the ones in NYC—Madison Square Garden, Irving Plaza, Bowery Ballroom, Brooklyn Bowl, the loft under Webster Hall, and Roseland Ballroom (RIP).

I loved NYC, but trying to navigate adulthood was chaotic for me. I barely knew how to be a child. I started college and was thrown into the world all on my own, with no idea what I was doing. You think you're an adult but you're really still a child. Still suffering from the discomfort of being in my own skin, I experienced immense social anxiety and was anxious about every move I made.

The transition from high school to college was weird. It wasn't hard, but it was strange. You go from being told what to do every second of every day to having complete freedom. I didn't know what to do with myself. I went from avoiding changing in the locker room to having to shower and poop with a bunch of people in a shared bathroom. I forced myself to go out and socialize. I sat on the quad with my headphones in until I, finally, met friends to drink with who had the same level of social anxiety as me.

Freshman year soon turned into one big blackout. My friends and I drank all of Thurfraturday (Thursday through Sunday). I had so much fun getting absolutely plastered at night, then sitting around the breakfast table the next morning laughing hysterically with my friends about the night before. Plus, drinking soothed my anxiety, and getting relief from that was pleasant. Even though I drank a little too much, I was able to keep my shit together. I would get hammered on Thursday night but still make it to my eight AM class on Friday.

College was the kind of place where you could skip class numerous times, bring a box of wine to class on the last day while handing in essays from all semester at once, and still get an A. Luckily, my core chemical engineering classes didn't start until my sophomore year. Freshman year, I had to get all my prerequisites out of the way, so I had some time to fug around. But many blackouts and one hospital trip later, I decided to focus a bit more on school.

I have always possessed an elemental sense of curiosity for how the world works, so I decided to study chemical engineering to try and understand it. I grasped chemistry and appreciated innovation. I think it started with playing with Legos as a child, having the urge and willingness to take things apart and put them back together. Chemistry is the building blocks of matter—it's what makes the world go around. For someone such as myself who was born with the innate desire to overanalyze and understand everything, I wanted to know everything about this system. I wanted to combine chemistry, math, technology, and biology to innovate and improve society and the planet.

Studying engineering made me think open-mindedly and innovatively. You're not going to explore those outer boundaries of your imagination without exterior assistance. You're not going to think outside the box by reading a textbook or following instructions in a lab manual. It takes projects requiring collaboration, communication, and different perspectives where you can test the limits of your potential and really explore the wavelengths of your brain. It is within engineering that these boundaries are limitless and can be explored.

Chemical engineers ("chemEs") can do anything. Ranging from food, beverages, drugs, and cosmetics to petroleum (what they bred us for in school). There is a chemical engineer designing everything you come in contact with—your home, the paint on your walls, the paper you use to blow your nose, the paper you use to wipe your butt, the canned food in your pantry, the medicine in your cabinets, the list goes on. A chemical engineer had a part to play in that object coming to fruition. I had a professor whose job was to design a sanitary napkin with maximum absorbency while still giving comfort and avoiding pad rash. My mistake was not asking him which brand to buy.

There will always be a need for engineers. We make life easier without anyone knowing what we do. We are the people behind the curtain who are responsible for society's operations. We combine math, chemistry, and physics to design profitable processes to mass produce chemicals to be used in everyday items, all while increasing efficiency, maintaining high purity, and decreasing capital and operating costs. We think on the atomic scale. We change the way atoms react with each other. We can manipulate matter and change the way a material behaves. We hold the universe in the palm of our hands. Who wouldn't want to do that?

The classmates I met through the program were some of the most intellectual, caring, and sophisticated humans I've met thus far. Each one of us had the fierce desire to succeed and the willingness to help our teammates get there. We knew that a burdensome program lay ahead, and we knew the only way to survive was to stick together. Everyone in the chemical engineering department grew very close very quickly and gave me a family feel like no other. We texted each other to check in on how the day was going, played sports together, met for coffee when we were having mental breakdowns, and stayed up all night studying for exams together. My classmates became my first solid support system.

We would be interviewing for the same job position while straightening each other's collars and tucking back each other's flyaway hair. There was always someone there to catch you if you needed help with homework, to find a mistake you made, to explain something you didn't understand—and, of course, to go out to the bar with you in the middle of the week. It was just who we were.

Some would deem us more of a cult because we had many events that were exclusive to the chemEs, including our own wing of the building with a private lounge and conference room. We hosted an annual Christmas party for the whole chemical engineering department. We wore matching ugly sweaters and showed up drunk. It was a great time to mingle and celebrate the success we had achieved the past semester. When we had to study or do an intense homework assignment, we would all take over the whole second floor computer lab in the library. We never intentionally kicked anyone out, but when we would be talking to each other across the room, we usually chased all the "non-chemEs" out.

I had the gracious opportunity, not only once, but twice, to study abroad. Grateful is an understatement. The first time was Mexico City, and the second was Dublin. Since the chemical engineering program had such a specific curriculum, we weren't able to do many study-abroad trips because the classes offered abroad were not on our roster. Our college administration organized a specific program just for the chemEs and sent one of our professors abroad with us to teach the program. We were set up in a school, with local students to mingle with. They took us around town, showed us the local spots, and taught us about their culture. Let me tell you, nothing will bond you harder than running around, getting drunk, and indulging in debauchery internationally with your friends. The secrets you share, the bonds you form, last like no others. Even if you don't talk every day down the road, that bond will forever remain intact, and the next time you see each other, you will pick things up as if you've never put them down.

While we felt like a family, there were times I felt I was on a different wavelength than my classmates—not in a bad way, of course. I've met some extraordinary people who will all do extraordinary things, but while my classmates were trying to get a six-figure job right out of college in the oil industry, I wanted no part of it. I was more concerned with what a GMO was and why there was fluoride in the drinking water when it's classified as a neurotoxin.

I was bored to tears taking plant design and couldn't use the software to save my life. I would sit there, one-on-one with the professor, to try to learn it but my brain didn't want to process it. However, while most of my classmates hated taking organic chemistry, I was a pro at it. I found it interesting, and I spoke its language. I wound up tutoring my classmates, demonstrating the beauty of teamwork. I learned that, personally, I was more interested in the actual chemistry rather than designing the equipment that mass-produces it, but I was not about to change my major and start all over. So, I persevered through it.

I worked on many different projects and did some broad research. The more I researched, the more I was turned off from entering the oil and gas industry. Even with "natural gas" being pushed as a safer, cleaner alternative, it's still polluting the ground water and destroying natural, balanced ecosystems. The conclusion I drew was that, if we absolutely have to do this, we must focus on remediating the pollution it's causing, but that wasn't part of the curriculum.

While we were being hired by these titans of industry to further develop GMOs, I was curious as to the damage being done to the body by consuming them. Our responsibility was to design new cosmetics, but I was wondering about the endocrine disrupters our bodies were being exposed to by applying it. While it was our job to make the next artificial sweetener, I was wondering what damage it would do to our gut health once consumed. While we were getting paid big money to design and construct new oil pipelines, I wanted to riot against them because they were destroying sacred Native American burial grounds. While everyone was trying to understand Big Oil's operations, I was wondering why we're drilling the Earth for oil when Mother Nature gave us everything we need above ground. I was curious as to why we weren't shifting away from their practices and finding alternatives, but no one was ready for that conversation. Excuse me for being another existential intellectual that did not want to contribute to the collapse of society.

To help avoid its collapse, we must shift from synthesizing oil and gas, poisoning the food industry, and polluting the water supply to recognizing and remediating the damage we've caused. This is only a mere fraction of what we need to do.

In addition to changing our actions, we must also shift our mindsets. People are so money-hungry, and they believe that's the root of happiness. News flash—you're not going to have anywhere to make and fight over money if we destroy the planet. Here we are, bleeding the Earth of its natural resources and decreasing its lifespan.

The new ages are here; it's time to adapt. We must move away from fossil fuels. We're releasing CO_2 into the air at an unsustainable rate, while simultaneously cutting down trees that convert the CO_2 back into O_2 and stabilize the temperature. CO_2 emissions are higher than they've ever been, and it's hotter than it's ever been. It will only increase unless we take action to halt and reverse the direction we are moving in. Don't even get me started on methane—we'll get to that one later.

Global warming is very real and very prominent, we are witnessing harsher hurricanes, and other natural disasters are becoming more extreme. The sea level is rising because water expands when it warms, and glaciers and ice sheets are melting. In the past four decades, sea levels have risen four inches. It's the industry's fault—the industry that has been paying more and more money to hide the consequences of their actions from the public eye. These corporate giants very well know the extent of their environmental impact, but they own most of the world's wealth, so they can apparently do whatever they want—including paying scientists to put out fake studies making their impacts seem much more subtle.

The industry needs a holistic, fundamental shift from fossil fuels to biofuels. It's going to take work and money, but it will be worth it in the end. The industry's so scared of hemp growing, even though it has proven benefits. It can grow to full size in five months and has stronger fibers and more nutrients than most other plants. Anything made from petroleum-based plastic can easily be replaced with hemp-based plastic, but corporations won't touch it because it's a Schedule I drug.

I was so turned off by the industry that I started to question my choice of studying chemical engineering. I had ample opportunities to travel with the chemEs to Texas to do oil refinery plant tours but couldn't bring myself to attend any of them. I would go to information sessions on campus when companies came for recruitment but subconsciously tune out the whole lecture. Even after a lifetime of ignoring my intuition, every cell in my body knew this wasn't the right path.

I wanted to create something that would benefit the Earth and its earthlings, something substantial to reverse the damage and restore our balance with nature so we may thrive collectively. At first, I wanted to work with medical marijuana and extract the active ingredient to treat inflammation, but I was shot down quickly by professors who wanted to chop my thought bubbles into squares. So, I picked a different plant and applied the same principles. I took the *Moringa oleifera* plant, put the plant matter into a distillation column, isolated the active ingredient that treated inflammation, and used it to treat a friend's liver ailment. Now, this was the type of chemical engineering I wanted to dedicate my time and energy to.

For another design project, my partner and I created a distillation column to extract the active ingredients from the stevia plant to use in place of sugar in several applications. This led me to dive deep into artificial sweeteners. I learned that digestion starts in the mouth, and when you consume artificial sweeteners, your body thinks it's going to receive actual sugar. Your body then produces the hunger hormone, ghrelin, that signals your body to consume sugar until it's satisfied. Once satisfied, the brain produces another hormone, leptin, which regulates fullness and signals your body to stop eating. Your body is tricked by the artificial sweetener and produces ghrelin when ingested, but when the body never receives actual sugar, it's never satisfied and doesn't turn on leptin. You find yourself craving to continue consuming it because the body has not been given the signal to stop eating. When I stood in front of my class and explained this, mouths dropped open. So many of us, even the smartest of the bunch, were still uneducated in so many ways.

While these projects excited me, I was still unsatisfied. I felt as though I was not making a big enough difference in the world. I wanted to help people, and I enjoyed studying science and math, so I became a tutor. So many students are turned off from subjects like chemistry and math because they think it's hard or don't understand it. I started tutoring math and chemistry to both high school and college students because I had a strong appreciation and under-standing of these subjects. I was able to break down these complex concepts into simple terms that students could understand. Nothing quite lit me up like seeing it finally click on their faces.

Helping others brought me joy, especially over interesting topics. I wanted to continue sharing my knowledge with those who were seeking to learn and, hopefully, further inspire them to study STEM for the right reasons. I wanted to inspire students to become ethical scientists, to change the future dynamics and current expectations of chemical engineers.

Chemical engineers have the building blocks of matter at their disposal. They have the power to manipulate matter, and they are using it to leak oil into clean drinking water and release toxic fumes into the air. I am fortunate and grateful for my education, but when we were learning how to fractionate ethylene instead of learning who Nikola Tesla was, there was a slight problem.

Chapter 4: Mother Goose

My life changed for the better when I met the chair of the chemical engineering department. All it took was her standing at the podium, radiating a strong presence, and explaining how shampoo and conditioner worked on a molecular level to inspire me. I wanted more of this woman in my life. Never have I ever seen a teacher so passionate about their students' experience. Most are just there to collect their paycheck and leave, and usually, when they get tenured, they stop caring. This one calculated how much money you would waste by skipping one lecture. And if you skipped class, she would take another student's phone and call you to find out where you were.

She so selflessly gave herself as an overflowing, abundant cup of knowledge for others to receive. She truly wanted to see us experience the best education possible to go off to work in the industry and make a difference in the world. Because our program was so exacting, and we spent so much time together, we looked up to her for support and guidance. She became our "Mother Goose". With her help, I began to realize my self-worth and discover my passions instead of just sitting through lectures and doing homework.

Her passion extended much further than just making sure we got a good education followed by a job. She wanted to make sure we truly understood everything we were taught in order to thrive in life. She taught us how to communicate effectively, in front of a crowd and with each other. She made us give presentations and public speeches to rooms full of people we didn't know. Yes, we hated it, but we thanked her for it. As we grow, it's not always comfortable. So, if it meant having to stand up on a stage in front of a class of forty people, getting critiqued on your public speaking while being scolded over the amount of times you said "um", so be it.

She went out of her way to make sure we had memorable experiences. If someone in our class was an athlete, under her orchestration, our whole class showed up to our teammates' sporting events wearing matching t-shirts she had made with the athlete's name on it. We all got up on a Saturday morning (some hungover, some not), put on the shirts, and went to the field to show our support for our classmate.

One of our classmates decided to join the priesthood instead of pursuing the industry. She made him a special book where we could all include our experiences with him. We each included a personal memory, letting him know how proud we were of him for pursuing this direction.

For graduation, she made us our own yearbook and took a group picture of us on the quad. She had special diploma frames made to hold our diploma on one side and our group picture on the other. To make it even more special, she had us sign everyone's frames on the matted section. She had set up all the frames down our exclusive chemE hallway, and we were crawling around on the floor, going down the line, signing each person's frame—hungover after formal, I might add. There was never a dull moment.

Mother Goose brought us all together and showed us what it meant to be a family. We had each other's backs. I was shown the importance of teamwork and how much farther you can go if you collaborate instead of compete against each other.

Then came interview day. "Everything is a test," Mother Goose told us. Our college was well-known for its engineering program, and many top corporate companies came to campus for recruitment. Mother Goose taught us everything we needed to know, from how to behave at recruitment sessions to how to interview to make them remember you and seek you out for employment. The previous graduating class had a 100 percent hiring rate right out of college because of her.

I had no idea how to even begin to prepare for an interview, so she was my saving grace. We were given fifty-plus behavioral questions for homework. First, we did them together, and later, we did them alone in the mirror. After we did them twenty times in the mirror, we did them twenty times more. Four hours might seem like a long time, but when it comes to investing in your future, it's comparable to pennies on the dollar. It's only the rest of your life.

We were drilled with interview practice. One classmate pretended to be the hiring manager while the other was the candidate. She held mock interview practices for us after class. Sometimes, they ran until nine PM on a Friday night, but what's worth more, a night wasted at the bar or an investment in your future?

We were taught how to effectively answer questions to show employers that we were problem solvers by using the STAR method —situation, task, action, resolution. They want to see how you effectively handle problems. So, for each answer, you would describe the situation and task at hand, the action you took to remediate the situation, and the outcome. Even if it wasn't your desired outcome, you could wield it into something you learned from. We were taught to always give an example.

She taught us that the recruiter will decide in the first ninety seconds whether they like you or not. We were taught to "play the game" and make a good impression. We had to walk in that room as if we were supposed to be there. She pointed out the importance of body language—everything from a firm handshake while making eye contact to smiling and introducing ourselves with confidence. Body language says a lot, and if you look timid, they're not going to take you seriously. If you're hunched over and slouching, you're not giving off an "I want this job" energy. When you're sitting up tall and maintaining good eye contact, you're showing them you're interested. No one is going to take you seriously if you can't walk into a room, look them in the eye, and give them a good handshake.

First impressions were everything when it came to interviewing. I was taught to take off all my earrings and jewelry (watch is fine). You don't want to sound like "Jingle Bells" when you're walking down the hallway into the interview room. We were taught to think of "funeral attire": black and white, match your belt with your sharp, shined shoes and starched shirt. When no one knew how to starch a shirt, she took us to the pharmacy and showed us exactly what to buy and how to apply it.

We were to have no nail polish on, except for a nude color or clear coat if you must. If you had red nail polish on, you had to take it off days before because it will stain your nail beds when you try to remove it. The girls were to tie their hair back and tuck in the flyaways. The boys had to shave their faces. I was taught that, while interviewing, you want to take away everything that would make you stand out so they focus solely on what you have to bring to their table. The interview is about your willingness to solve problems and get the job done. When you get the job, you can start wearing jewelry to work, grow a beard, and dye your hair whatever color you want.

After we entered the room and greeted them with our strong handshake, we were to hand them our résumé, even if they already had one in front of them. We were to hand them a fresh résumé, printed on résumé paper, obviously, all in a résumé folder, obviously. I didn't even know what a résumé folder was until I met Mother Goose. You can buy them at any stationary supply store.

We had to come up with an elevator pitch about ourselves—a short introduction that would take less than two minutes. Small talk is always good; make silly little connections that they'll remember you by—whether it's through some hometown connection or through sports, music, or other media. It's good to talk about things other than straight interview questions at first. You'll be more relaxed, and your conversation will just flow.

We were led to believe we could get a job at these major corporations and be able to change them from the inside out, but only after we'd nailed the interview and accepted a job offer. To do so, we were taught to research the company beforehand to know all about their operations. The interviewer will always ask if you have any questions for them at the end. We were taught to have at least two questions to ask to show that we did our research: the more specific, the better. You want to make an impression.

At the end of the interview, always ask for their business card; then, send them a follow-up email with a brief thank-you no more than two days after the interview. If you made any connections with your small talk, this is where you would include them to remind the interviewer of who you were. You will be surprised how far small talk can get you.

Now, this is the type of education I didn't mind paying for—advice that would take me far in life.

So, I took out all seven of my eight earrings, only because I physically couldn't get the last one unhinged. Mother Goose met me in the hallway before the interview. While straightening my collar and fixing my hair, the first thing she said to me was, "I thought you were going to take out all of your earrings." Totally saw that one coming.

I saw the prior candidate walk out of the interview office. He was in a suit and tie—but with an electric blue shirt underneath and long, dyed hair, and an earring in his right ear. Mother Goose had clearly not trained this one. Game over; I had this in the bag.

I thought my interview went well. I hit all the social cues, gave thorough answers to every one of their questions, and asked them questions at the end, but all I could think about was the earring that was still in my ear. Later that night, after some rubbing alcohol and a lot of pulling and tugging, I got my last earring undone, but not until after the interview. So, if that's the reason I'm not working at one of the largest global cosmetic companies right now, I'll take it. I wouldn't be able to test on animals anyway.

Because I didn't get the job, Mother Goose had set up a one-on-one meeting to help navigate the fate of my career. She asked me, "So, what do you want to do with your life?" Is there a scarier question? "Save the world and continue learning," I said. I answered from the heart, not thinking about making money to survive in this capitalist narrative only designed for the top one percent to thrive.

I was so consumed with hatred and grief for the state of the world that I decided I wanted to dedicate my career to doing what I could to help improve our living conditions in a sustainable way. I knew I wanted to stick with chemical engineering because it was more than just oil and gas, even if that's what they were breeding us for in school. I was able to work on projects that sparked my interests and passions, but my mind kept on coming back to the havoc these industrial practices were wreaking on our bodies and environment.

What I wanted was persistent intellectual stimulation, not to be stuck pushing papers behind a desk full-time. I didn't want to do one thing for the rest of my life. I wanted to touch upon several different projects and travel all over the place. I wanted to do something worthwhile and leave a tangible impact on the world. But at that point, I was just trying to survive college.

Chapter 5: Addicted to Dissociating to a Higher Dimension

I tried to focus more on my studies but had trouble concentrating. I would be sitting there, trying to read, but my brain would be somewhere else thinking of what I saw on the internet that morning, spiraling over what I did when I blacked out, or playing show tunes from something I hadn't watched in years. I found it near impossible to sit down to try and study.

Many coffees and cigarettes later, I could no longer handle what was in front of me. I tried a tutor but was more confused. I tried office hours but just sat there focusing on the social aspects of the situation, overthinking the right amount of eye contact to make or whether I had shaken their hand hard enough, and not one word stuck. I started spiraling again over whether this curriculum was for me. But apparently, not being able to focus at college is common, and fellow students handed out ADHD meds like candy.

The first time I took one, it was like turning a radio station from static to in-tune. It quelled all my distractions and racing thoughts. I was able to read without my mind wandering off. It allowed me to slow myself down and focus *and finish* solely what was in front of me, which is ironic because I was eating prescribed amphetamine salts, but whatever this was, I needed it.

If someone had followed me around with a camera the first time I took those meds, it would like the beginning of the movie *Limitless*, where he finally cleans his apartment and starts to get his life together. I cleaned my whole dorm room, did laundry, and even put all my clothes away. People underestimate how having clutter around you clutters your mind. You ever clean your room thoroughly, then you can focus and get work done? It feels fantastic.

The knots in my brain untangled themselves. I was able to sit down and do my physics homework. Not only was I able to focus on it, but I was also able to understand it for the first time. I was able to sit through tutorial videos without giving up after the first few minutes. Plus, my penmanship was prestigious and I made myself food instead of eating peanut butter out of the jar. (Whoever needs to hear this, you're not going to come back to the peanut butter knife. Don't leave it on the counter. Just put it in the sink/dishwasher.)

Besides the euphoria I experienced from my brain functioning correctly for the first time in my life, I felt as if I'd gotten hit by a train the next day. Since the medication completely quelled my appetite, I didn't eat any food, just smoked cigarettes. I didn't drink any water, only coffee. But I had an exam coming up and a lab report due and more physics to learn, so I took another.

My drinking habits increased exponentially while being cracked out on amphetamines. I was unable to get drunk, so I had to drink more and wound up blacking out quickly. Yes, I know mixing the two was a toxic cocktail for my liver to process, but this was college, and we did what we had to do to survive.

Because I was smart, when I complained about not being able to pay attention, people just said, "You can do it. You're smart!" Yes, I know I am intelligent, but I also lack executive function. Part of me is grateful for my lack of diagnosis in childhood. Little kids in class-rooms that have trouble sitting still, difficulty waiting their turn, and uncontrollable, random outbursts are being diagnosed with ADHD.

The doctor's conclusion is to have these hyperactive children micro-dose amphetamines to calm down. Make it make sense. At least our inattentiveness saved us from all the propaganda being spoon-fed to us in school.

I had trouble focusing in grade school but never really took it into consideration because I was blessed with a photographic memory and motivated by fear. Engineering was different, though. You couldn't pass with a photographic memory. It required critical thinking, and my paralyzed, traumatized brain was stuck in freeze mode and had a hard time adapting.

I started to receive failing grades and panicked. I needed help, so I let myself go on medication. I despise Big Pharma and believe they are knowingly poisoning people, so it was hard for me to surrender and take it, but I struggled pretending everything was fine. I hated to think of relying on outside substances to get my work done, but I did it anyway. I allowed myself to take what I needed to do what I needed to get done. I found a psychiatrist, and as soon as I described my inability to focus while reading, it was a done deal.

After getting a proper diagnosis from a psychiatrist and learning more about the symptoms of ADHD, I finally felt understood by someone. Even if I was paying them to listen to me, I didn't feel as lost. So many of my patterns and behaviors started to make sense. It's why I either focused on too many things at once or dove into one topic ruthlessly; I knew no balance between. It's why I created doom piles that stayed there so long, I eventually threw them into bags and into a closet and forgot about them forever, or at least until I needed that one random thing I couldn't find. It was why I ignored my bills until they sent at least three notices and threatened to send me to the collection agency. It was why I let all those bags of spinach wilt in the fridge even though I swore it would be different this time. It was why I experienced panic, yet possessed no ability to get up and do some-thing about it. It explained why I felt like I was continuously busy, yet achieving nothing.

Having ADHD is an enduring battle between you and your

thoughts while pretending you're okay all the time. I was unmotivated unless there was a time crunch. Procrastinating, yet having a fear of failure, is a dangerous place to be. Even when there was a deep, subtle panic from doing nothing, I continued to do nothing. I would have a long to-do list but lacked the ability to get out of bed. I saved everything I wanted to read online to my reading list but never read any of it. I eventually gave up and returned to the endless doom-driven scroll for the false sense of dopamine.

I would try to read a paragraph of a book but have to keep rereading it because my mind would wander off. Before I knew it, more than twenty minutes had passed, and I was only half a page in. More often than not, I gave up trying to finish it. I think I'm in the middle of every book I've ever started.

I faced the repeated cycle of coming up with a project, telling everyone about it, buying supplies for it, then doing it once or twice and not carrying it through. I put off minuscule tasks even though they would take fifteen minutes to complete and needed an hour break after. I was always tired in the morning and throughout the day but, somehow, found the energy to be productive at night. I was finally ready to get off the couch and conquer the day at eight PM, wanting to magically fix everything that was wrong in my life overnight.

I didn't want to always ask questions in class because, half of the time, I wasn't paying attention. I didn't want to dig myself a deeper hole. I quietly sat on the sidelines and pretended to know what was going on. I crammed everything into my brain days before the test and forgot everything right after.

Cue imposter syndrome, getting praised but still feeling like a failure. Getting compliments makes you feel awkward, and you're inclined not to accept them. You know you understand a wealth of knowledge but, at the same time, feel like you know nothing.

I started to get annoyed with myself and beat myself up over not being able to follow society's norms. I asked myself: *Why couldn't I do anything without a deadline? Why couldn't I simply function? Why did I struggle with things others did with ease?*

I didn't know it at the time, but I struggled fitting in because I was put here to create something new. I needed to step back and give myself more credit because it took a lot of work to get me where I was.

After stepping back, I began to realize there were advantages to having ADHD as well. We're able to come up with new strategies to overcome setbacks and carry on stronger than ever. We're naturally curious and ask the questions no one else thinks of because we don't think the way anyone else does. We are the kind of people who come up with big-picture ideas. We just have trouble deploying them due to lack of executive function, but this is why we must work as a team.

We have a great sense of humor and use it to cope with difficult situations. Our self-deprecating humor shows the world we are not perfect, and it's normal. We make others feel more comfortable with not being perfect, and that is a gift.

We are masters of creating our own reality because we're always daydreaming. Our creativity excels—use this to your advantage. More people with ADHD need to pursue science; there's a nook and cranny for everything your brain wants to hyper-fixate on. The euphoria the mad scientist experiences while falling in love with all the unknown and undiscovered parts of the universe tops all.

Our brains are all wired differently, and unfortunately, some of us have unbalanced brain chemistry. I didn't want to be on meds forever, just until I balanced myself out. Medication affects everyone differently, and while I fiercely believe you can heal yourself naturally, sometimes you need a little chemical crutch to pull yourself out of a chemical imbalance.

We are too hard on ourselves, and we shouldn't feel shame or embarrassment. We must shift the narrative and applaud ourselves for giving ourselves what we need. If you need it, you need it. It may not be forever; it may just be a crutch. If you struggle without it, love yourself enough to give yourself what you need. Love yourself enough also to not settle on the first pill you're prescribed if it doesn't work.

There were times when I didn't want to take the medicine because of how it made my body feel, but I had work to do. I was hesitant to take it at times, but every time I did, I questioned my hesitance because the medication made me feel great once it kicked in. I was productive, my thoughts were in a better place, and I was losing weight.

Once I started losing weight, that and school became my focus. I would do what I had to do to make that number on the scale keep decreasing. I became a bit obsessed with watching that number drop, to a point where I was stepping on the scale five times a day. I would get mad when the number fluctuated, even though I knew that my weight could easily fluctuate around five pounds a day.

While the medication helped me get my work done, I grew to a point where it further contributed to my chemical imbalance than helped it. My quality of sleep had substantially diminished, and I had absolutely no appetite, so I tried to compensate by smoking weed. Weed was the Band-Aid for my reality. My mental health was down so low I would get high just to stay grounded. Once the meds wore off, I was crying, for no reason, almost every night. I was making impulsive, irrational decisions without thinking clearly and experiencing bouts of depression. But as soon as I popped a pill, that all disappeared—until the pill wore off again. I hated to rely on them and wanted so desperately to be able to function off them, but I wasn't able to get any work done unless I took them now.

I let myself believe I was not worthy of achievement because I couldn't do it without stimulants. Meanwhile, there were many people out there without brain stimulants who were half as smart as I was, making substantial moves in life simply because they had confidence in themselves.

Even on the medication, I was not functioning as well as others were. I was zoning out, conscious I was zoning out, and then shaming myself for it. My negative thoughts only brought in more negativity.

Tripping over the vacuum I left out, moving the doom pile of clothes back and forth from the chair to the bed for days, forgetting about laundry in the machine and having to rewash it—I was forgetting things everywhere. The real walk of shame is when you have to walk back into a room for the third time because you keep forgetting why you went in there. There were so many minutes of self-blame.

Instead of blaming ourselves, we must be compassionate to ourselves when we make mistakes like this. We've been shamed enough by outside figures—we don't need to contribute to it as well. We must train our brains to operate differently; no more replaying corrupted scenarios in our heads. We need to let that go. We must be kinder to ourselves and give ourselves what we need to function properly. Your ADHD can be a blessing in disguise. You have the ability to see things differently and connect the dots others can't.

Mental illness causes such exasperation, and it's not acknowledged or dealt with in the correct way. Doctors must take precautions —proper therapy, diagnosis, and treatment—without thinking about the check Big Pharma is going to cut after they write that prescription. There are fundamental flaws in the system preventing people from getting the help they need. Trying to battle the flaws in the system while simultaneously battling your declining mental health is exhausting. We're ignored when we say we need help until we feel so helpless and lost that we do something irrational; only then do people notice.

ADHD is the epitome of chemical imbalance, but would you believe some people say it's a made-up disease? Our brains fail to produce and transmit the correct levels of dopamine and serotonin, and people just call us lazy. ADHD is a battle against yourself. It's the constant battle between wanting all your stuff organized and completed but telling yourself you will do it later. It's a constant battle with not wanting to take your meds, but as soon as you take them, you're glad you did. It's a battle between you and your intrusive thoughts that consume you.

The best way I learned to manage my ADHD was to become

educated on it. I had a lot of questions as to how I ended up like this. After engaging in further sessions with a psychiatrist, I came to learn that symptoms of ADHD can stem from repressed trauma—like procrastination. Are we really lazy or just stuck in freeze mode? Do we really have trouble learning? Or are we hyperactive because our brains have been trained to always be on the alert from repeated exposure to dangerous situations?

We're criticized for our actions instead of being taught how to manage them. Our brains are operating in a hyperactive state. Instead of training them to slow down, we're getting mad and attacking ourselves because our brains don't function normally. We make impulsive decisions, doomscroll, drink alcohol, and eat trash because we are chasing artificial dopamine due to our brains not producing it naturally. Once we become aware of this, we can learn how to reroute ourselves to remediate our pernicious actions.

Actions we took to keep us safe in childhood are ruining us as adults. It is difficult to unlearn this behavior and adopt new ways, but once we do, we will thrive. It doesn't happen overnight. We may slip up and fall into our old ways, but what matters is how we pick ourselves up, dust ourselves off, and get back out on the playing field. Sure, we might need a day in bed here or there, and we must respect the need for rest and recovery. What we're doing takes a large emotional toll, and it's exhausting.

After growing sick and enervated from the effects the medication had on my body, I began to research alternative ways of managing ADHD. I incorporated exercise, eliminated certain foods from my diet, and even tried meditating. For some, meditation can help with overall well-being. For others, they cannot even fathom the thought because their brains are working so fast, they skip letters while writing.

Meditation was hard for me because I had too many thoughts bouncing around my brain. What helped me manage my racing thoughts best was writing them all down. Writing allowed me to calm my hyperactive mind so I could explore the depths of the emotional territory I was avoiding. Writing allowed my racing thoughts to exit my brain, to be left on the paper to make room for the things that needed to stick. It saved me. For most things, if I had to remember them, I had to write them down, right then and there. If not, I would lose them forever. There was no room in my brain to take in new information.

It doesn't have to be writing, though. Find what works for you, but you must have the courage to explore. It can be anything; find a hobby to do, learn an instrument, make something—paintings, jewelry—fugging color an adult coloring book. We have all this pent-up energy, and we must channel it into something constructive that we enjoy doing.

It turns out when we actually take care of ourselves, like exercising to release endorphins and not eating processed junk, we actually feel better. Yeah, I know it's the last thing you want to hear. It's the last thing we want to do, but what we desire most is often waiting for us on the other side of what we are avoiding.

Eating handfuls of shredded cheese out of the bag isn't going to cut it anymore. If you eat garbage, you're going to feel like garbage. They weren't lying when they said, "You are what you eat." You must take diet and exercise into consideration, or you're not really giving yourself a fair chance.

You don't have to identify yourself with your mental illness. You don't have to be embarrassed about taking medication. It is demonized, yet promoted by society. Stop letting society's opinions influence your decisions. You need to do what's best for you. You may need it for a few years, or you may need it for the rest of your life. Love and honor yourself enough to give your body what it needs without caring what people think. If you don't care what others think, congratulations. You're one step closer to taking back your power.

Chapter 6: Take a Chower, Chine Your Choes

I still had two years of school left and lots of work to be done, but it was summertime now, and all my friends just happened to be staying around campus. They were either working on campus or living in apartments off-campus and decided not to go home over the summer.

I had quite the best possible group of friends at college—the solid, blunt, ride-or-die friends you need in life. We partied together, evaded the cops together, ate psychedelics together, laughed, cried, survived the chemical engineering program, and left a legacy around town. What better people could you ask for?

We found the weirdest things to funnel beer out of, including plastic baseball bats and a plastic target hunting duck. There was never a dull moment—it was always a rager. We even joined our local bar's dart league and played against other local bars around town. It was team bonding at its finest.

For some completely random reason, we started saying every word beginning with "sh" with a "ch". It started with "chit" and quickly morphed into "chirt", "chave", then "take a chower, chine your choes". It was catchy, and soon we were all saying it and couldn't stop. The more you say it, the catchier it gets. My personal favorite was "CHHH". It's way more deliverable than "shhhh".

We threw the craziest parties and always managed to get the cops called. We had the only backyard on the block, and it was surrounded by apartment buildings. At any given time, there were hundreds of people looking down on us, witnessing our debauchery. So many times, you could barely move around in that backyard because of the crowd of people present.

It was on the most populated street around college. You could walk outside and take your pick of which bar or bodega to enter. It was right in the middle of all the commotion, so you didn't miss a beat.

I spent most of my time in an Irish Pub-Café down the block. It was an Irish pub that looked like it was taken straight out of Temple Bar. It was the most well-mixed melting pot I've ever been a part of. It attracted the most interesting, eclectic, wayward souls. Everyone came from different backgrounds, and all had something to teach each other. They did not overpack it with underclassmen for the sake of making money. It was a black hole; it sucked you in and made it impossible to leave. I had to pass it walking home from class and always got sucked in. Next thing I knew, I was sending "U Up?" texts at three PM.

From drinking coffee and sitting at a picnic table outside doing schoolwork, to eating psychedelics and watching the local artwork melt, the pub was filled with people who were intellectually stimulating and could hold a conversation. The people I met there gave me advice I carry with me to this day. They teach you the chit you won't learn in the classroom, even getting a chemical engineering degree. I learned what numerology was and how they actually treat the chickens you buy at the grocery store when they're still alive. You met people who could hold space for you to talk to them about your problems, who would buy you drinks so you would keep talking. It was like a therapy session and a fulfilling night out, all in one.

Another friend I met in there, told me to "slow the fug down" in all aspects of my life, which was ironic because the conversation was taking place over a pile of uppers and bottles of champagne. I was operating at a thousand mph and going too hard, too fast. I had no self-awareness and was just trying to survive. It quite possibly saved my life because there was a point where I didn't think I was going to make it to graduation. He saw right through my confidence issues and told me to stop selling myself short. He was my first friend to stop stepping on eggshells and give me a reality slap in the face. He also told me to always run clean at work—afterward is the time to party— and there are times when it's good to be a dickhead. He taught me to chase my passions instead of waiting for something to fall into my lap. I wouldn't be where I am today without that advice.

The bartenders were always there to talk to me and give me advice about my boy troubles, telling me how when you tell boys you like them, they don't know what to do, so they get scared and run away. They always pointed me away from the fugboys, also saving my life. They made me a bodega birthday cake (a BEC with a candle in it) and didn't even get mad at me when I blacked out and stole a fake plant. I woke up the next morning, hungover and confused, and brought it back. They welcomed me with open arms and chots of whiskey.

They hosted open mic nights every Tuesday where my friends and I would play music and clean the bar out of Lagunitas. One night, while sipping down an ice-cold one, I heard someone playing "Blue in the Face" by Alkaline Trio. Whoever was playing it, had a great voice and even added in his own little vocal interjections. I was smitten. I was surprised, and excited, to hear this song being played because few people I knew had any idea who that band was, so I darted inside to see who it was. I had went over and congratulated him on his song choice and performance.

His name was Connor and we instantaneously formed a connection. Whether it was our shared love of the same music, drinking, or trauma-dumping on each other before we even knew what trauma-dumping was, we became very close very quickly. We were basically the same person. I didn't know if this was a good or a bad thing at the time, but we were friends now.

He would change the course of my life forever.

He was from New Jersey, but he was the most-New-York New Jersey kid I knew. There was not a time where he was not wearing a Yankees or Rangers jersey or hat. He loved New York much more because of all the obvious reasons from the previous chapter. Both of his parents went to our college and met there, so New York City held a special place in his heart.

He was the type of person who had a strong personality some could only handle in small doses. Not me, though—I couldn't get enough. It took a special kind of tough to break down that rough exterior, but under it was a heart of gold.

I loved him deeply, like family. He met me on my weird emotional wavelength and liked the same emo bands I did. I will always remember blasting music in his apartment and hanging out on his balcony that overlooked our territory. We threw keg parties, cooked big pasta dinners for us and all his roommates, smoked on the rooftop, drew pictures, and played music. We had a lot of fun together.

He was super creative and wrote his own music. He was the one who gave us the term "fug"—giving credit where credit is due. I liked it because it's less vulgar than its curse-word counterpart, and I was trying to watch my potty mouth. We were both genuinely creative and always writing something down. For him, it was music. For me, it was words to calm my racing thoughts. We were both fiercely cranking out words on the notes app on our phones at any given moment.

He loved music and would play live shows all over the city. We drove my family's minivan back and forth to his house in New Jersey to get all his music equipment and took it around the city, setting up shows. I was there when he was writing his music. I was there to help him set up and break down every show. He was very talented and always put on a spectacular performance. I helped him get the ball rolling with his music, so I just hoped he kept with it.

We motivated each other to go to the gym and always made sure we made it to class in the morning after a night of drinking. We helped each other clean our apartments and do all the dishes when it was our turn. Even though we had different majors, we would sit next to each other and do homework together. He helped me do my Chinese homework, and he didn't even take the class. There were some days we wanted to tear each other's hair out, but there was always a deeper sense of love there. Are they really your best friend if they don't make you want to tear their fugging hair out?

We were strictly platonic (I know you're wondering). He was way too volatile, and I knew that commencing a romantic relationship would not be good for my mental health. I couldn't even look at myself naked in the mirror at the time, so there was no room for a boyfriend. I could open up sexually to someone only if I was wasted, didn't know them, and didn't have to see them again.

Everyone who knew Connor knew he liked to drink beer, that he played music, and that his sister was addicted to heroin. He was very up-front about it. It brought him great pain, and it didn't take long for him to open up about it. You could see how affected he was, but he didn't let it stop him from carrying on in life.

He was a go-getter; if he wanted something, he would find a way to make it his. There was something to be admired, yet feared, about his ambition. He went out of his way to make things happen and talk to people. He could walk in and out of a place with a job or a show booked. He would always say thank you and let you know how much he appreciated whatever you did for him, but he could talk you into doing whatever he wanted.

He was also my first lesson with setting boundaries for myself. He was good at business and making deals but always wanted some-thing out of it. And I, with my inability to say "no" due to being a people-pleaser raised on transactional love, always gave it to him. It was bad enough with the alcohol, but—including all the other substances we abused together, including each other—it was a recipe for disaster.

He had a rather addictive personality and would always indulge in substances at an exorbitant rate, where I was able to pick up things and put them down when I reached my threshold (except alcohol). There was no picking up something and putting it down for him. It needed to be finished.

Being friends with him taught me a lot about myself. He was like a mirror to my personality in some ways. We both liked to drink to excess, and we did. We were both burying demons we didn't talk about. Both our lives had been affected by the same external factors so closely already. At some points, we brought out the worst in each other. But we were in the same boat, and we helped each other survive college.

We loved each other but were detrimental to each other.

It was a harsh lesson to learn about how the two can be confused.

My friends and I spent the rest of the summer running around the city like deviants—playing darts all over the city, getting plastered and hitting bull's-eyes, stealing more fake plants from different bars. We had friends passing out with their shoes on and waking up covered with permanent marker drawings. We found other friends passed out under newspapers like homeless people in the middle of the street.

We went to a three-hour, all-you-can-drink special at the bar down the street from school and purposefully didn't eat to get as fugged up as we could. We even left in the middle, went down the street to a friend's apartment, did a snowbank of uppers off an iPad, and went back to the bar to keep drinking. I was so fugged up I tried to take a whole pitcher of beer out of the bar to bring it home. I got caught by the bouncer and didn't make it home with the pitcher. We went home and continued the day drinking Rich Lokos (Four Loko lemonade + forty-ounce Miller High Life) and always ended our nights at our favorite Irish Pub-Café.

Chapter 7: Better Living Through Chemistry

Now I'm not a doctor, and this is not medical advice, but for those of you thinking about dabbling in entheogenic medicine for healing purposes, I can tell you it can be very therapeutic. Of course, you need the right dose, headspace, and environment, but if done under the right conditions, it can be a profoundly transforming experience.

It's true that you can get to the same headspace through breathwork and meditation, but my neurodivergent brain was already used to external stimuli, so this worked for me.

I fell in love with life for the first time after consuming entheogens. I saw how beautiful this world can be, and for the first time, I actually started to feel good. I laughed like I'd never laughed before. I started to gain a real sense of appreciation for people and experiences in my life. I started to become in tune with my soul and drop into my body for the first time. But above all, I started to question everything.

Oh, chit. I said with a giggle.

This is amazing!
I love my friends!
What am I doing here?
Do I really want to be a chemical engineer?
This is amazing!
Look at this grass!
The clouds are dancing!
Oh my god, the world is fugged.
Oh my god, the world is simultaneously so beautiful!
I can see why this is a catalyst for many mental revolutions.

It silenced my anxieties. It was a one-way ticket to connecting with my higher self. It quelled all the extra thoughts bouncing around my head that my ADHD meds couldn't. The little voice inside my head that was previously muffled was louder than ever, and all I could hear was, "I better start taking care of myself, mind, body, and soul. No one's coming to save me. I have to do it myself."

It was the exact psychedelic slap in the face from the universe that I needed. It heightened all of my senses and I started to notice things I was never conscious of before, and this lasted way after the comedown. I was now awake to the fact I needed to start taking care of my body. My social anxiety just kind of melted away, and things that bothered me before didn't even cross my mind after. I had different things to worry about now.

I was able to think about what was troubling me and bringing me pain and accept it with compassion rather than guilt and shame. I was able to face my fears directly with a level head. It silenced all the white noise in my mind and made my intuitive voice become abundantly clear.

It gave me a sense of empowerment and changed my mindset. I was able to look at my mind, body, and soul and accept it with love and grace. It made me more inclined to feel the feelings I'd been suppressing over the years. It worked better than any type of medication I took. I was moving forward with a renewed sense of freedom; it was time to get to work.

Like I said, I'm not a doctor, but I am a chemical engineer. And by understanding chemistry, engineering, and the industry, I've learned a bit about how the world operates. The same people who want to call us drug addicts for using these types of "drugs" as healing tools are the same ones who are drinking alcohol, consuming excessive amounts of processed sugar daily, eating factory-farmed meat full of hormones and antibiotics, watching porn, and believing everything the news/media tells them. Other people's perspectives of you are simply a reflection of themselves.

Dabbling in entheogens allowed me to start the long journey of healing the hurt that was consuming me. I had adopted some bad habits throughout my college career. I had a demanding curriculum, and lots of work to do, and I had to get it done no matter the expense to my well-being. I was young, and my body was invincible.

I started becoming more intentional with my health and conscious of what I was putting into my body. My go-to meal changed from fried chicken tenders with fries to avocado sourdough toast with turmeric and black pepper. (The compounds in black pepper increase the bioavailability of the active ingredients in turmeric that treat inflammation and the microorganisms in sourdough are great for your gut health.) I started to focus on more balanced meals and protein intake. I drank a lot of water, green tea, took B_{12} every day, and started to go to the gym. I started incorporating yoga multiple times a week. (There's free yoga all over NYC). I felt really good after doing it. My head was clear, and it put me in a better mood. I wanted to go back to do it again.

Breakfast was still an iced coffee and a loosie from the bodega. Lunch was prescribed amphetamine salts and—maybe—a granola bar. Dinner was avocado toast or a turkey sandwich and then however much alcohol would put me to sleep—until I was malnourished and cranky and had to sleep for days straight to balance myself out. But hey, all my homework was turned in on time, and I was passing my exams.

I was often pulling all-nighters in the library. It was quiet, and I could focus with no distractions. On those nights, dinner was more prescribed amphetamine salts. Always cigarettes and more iced coffee. Sometimes water, sometimes forgetting.

I started to become aware of the changes I had to make, but stubborn me wanted to change everything overnight. I wanted it to happen right away, not yet knowing that substantial change happens slowly and steadily.

I still had a bad relationship with food and would eat whatever was in front of me to get it over with. Many times, I stood in my kitchen eating handfuls of nuts while I tried to think of something else to make until I had eaten so many I was no longer hungry. I made sandwiches in the cafeteria and brought them back to my dorm room and ate alone and quickly to get it over with. I was a mess, but I was on a mission to get better.

I was always stepping on the scale. Checking the scale is like checking your phone—not needed multiple times a day, but we can feel compelled to do it anyway. As the number on the scale continued to go down, my mission to lose a hundred pounds started to intensify. I would do anything to see that number decrease—skipping meals, over-exercising, trying over-the-counter supplements I read about online.

I started using my ADHD medication for energy to work out and wound up doing mindless cardio on the machines in the gym until I burned seven-hundred-something calories, not paying attention to my body telling me to stop. I learned that when you exercise, body fat gets converted to water and CO_2, and you lose it through sweating and breathing, so I did a lot of cardio. The meds quelled my appetite, but after many prescribed amphetamine binges, my body desperately tried to hold onto any food I would eat, and I wound up gaining weight right back. I was at war with myself but determined to reach my goal.

So, I did it. I exercised, did yoga, and ate differently until I lost a hundred pounds. After achieving my goal, something shifted in me, and I no longer cared about the number on the scale. I barely stepped on the scale after that, but I still didn't feel as good as I wanted to. I was proud of myself for reaching my goal because I had never done something that substantial before, but gripping fists full of empty fabric and looking in the mirror naked, I still wasn't satisfied. I was still anxious over my appearance and did not feel well. I felt better than I did when I was a hundred pounds heavier but, somehow, still like chit. Nothing will quite rip us apart like ourselves in front of a mirror, illuminating every imperfection, picking at our faces, furthering our scars.

The battle you go through with the sacred human vessel that's holding you is different for everyone, yet somehow the same—never being satisfied and constantly searching for ways to alter your appearance, ignoring your health and safety measures. Fat people want to be slimmer, skinny people want to be slimmer, and sometimes, skinny people want to be bigger. People go under the knife and spend tons of money altering their physical appearance. Is anyone comfortable in their body?

We spend childhood wanting to be adults. Now, we're spending adulthood wishing we were children again. We judge ourselves the same way those who hurt us most judged us. We repeat the hurtful words to ourselves that we heard growing up, and we believe them to be true. Now, we're all adults with the mindsets of children. We've let adjectives become insults that ruined our lives, and now suffer from a low sense of self-worth. It shouldn't be this way. It doesn't need to be this way. It's not going to be this way. We must start being nicer to ourselves and love ourselves shamelessly. May we move forward, building a healthier self-image.

I began to change the narrative and developed a sense of appreciation for my body. It had gotten me this far in life and I was blessed and grateful to be where I was. I was starting to take care of my body by fueling it with what it needed. I was aspiring to feel good instead of solely looking good, and life improved.

My immense anxiety started to dissipate once I grew to appreciate my body, but I couldn't get my mind off how strategically twisted the industry was and grew increasingly appalled. I experienced college and learned how beautiful life can be, and at the same time, I realized how society is blindly enslaving us.

I started freshman year eating processed junk food and went into senior year gaining an appreciation for food and the nourishment it provides your body. I learned how vital its intake is. I learned the effect food has on our consciousness, how everything we put in our body either fights or fuels sickness, how different pH levels affect the body, and what foods trigger an inflammatory response.

I grew passionate about wanting to know how every ingredient on that label affected the body. After learning so much, I was embarrassed by the chit I used to put into my body (some men included). We're reading ingredients now.

As my undergraduate college career was winding down, I was celebrating my success in my favorite Irish Pub-Café, exchanging random information with other people in there. As I was teaching people how to sternly shake hands like Mother Goose had taught us, an idea popped into my head. I wanted to collect all the loose Post-it notes that were my thoughts and compile them into a self-help book for people to read. I wanted to share my experience with others who were on the same journey and needed help.

I had been through a lot in my short lifespan, with my weight loss journey and everything I learned about chemical engineering and communications. I knew I would have to ask Mother Goose's permission to share her information, and that night, in divine timing, who did I see entering as I was exiting? None other than Mother Goose! I pitched her my idea, and she thought it was excellent. She said absolutely and told me how excited she was. After that encounter, I knew this was the move I had to make.

I started researching and writing more and more and found

myself enjoying it. I loved writing; it helped alleviate my stress and gave intention to everything I did. I knew I wanted to write to share my experiences and help people. I am writing to help you so you can help yourself. I'm not here to save you—only you can do that. I'm here to share how I did it and help you along your journey.

To change and heal ourselves collectively, change must start at the individual level. It's time we start caring about each other and being more compassionate to those we share the planet with. It's bigger than our individual egos.

You learn a lot when you're willing to open your mind. You learn how to actually play this game called life rather than just letting it happen to you. I have been blessed with the places I have been able to travel to and spend time in, the education I received, and the incredible connections I've made along the way. I am so grateful for the friends I've made and the conversations I have been fortunate to have. It was time to put it all to use.

Chapter 8: Tried It Once, but It Wasn't Enough ...

I survived the rest of senior year and flew away from the comfy Hobbit hole that was undergraduate college. I landed back at my parents' house and right into my first full-time job. That's what college was preparing us for, right? Wrong.

I had a harder transition going from college to working full-time than from high school to college. College doesn't prepare you for the real world. It teaches you it's okay to be a drunk fool and to skip out on your commitments. Going from that to working full-time was a real culture shock. You couldn't skip work like you could skip class and get away with it because you weren't feeling good or wanted to nap.

I landed in a small, filthy warehouse in "upstate" New York, helping manage the environmental health and safety compliance for a manufacturing plant producing wholesale rubber conveyor belts. They operated twenty-four hours over three shifts, so no downtime. Working full-time was like being stuck in the library, studying for hours without being able to take a break. Staring at a computer for eight hours a day while your eyes degrade and your back contorts will really fug you up.

I started consuming sugary coffees to stay awake all day and began gaining weight back that I had worked so hard to lose. I went from taking 10,000 steps before noon, walking around the city, to sitting in a chair all day. There was no place to walk around unless you wanted to walk out onto the plant floor, but the air quality was horrible, so I stayed in the office. You couldn't walk through the plant without brushing up against something and raw carbon dust turning your clothes and skin black. It was difficult to breathe out on the warehouse floor because they were using known carcinogens as adhesive agents and not wearing breathing protection. Part of my job was to get them all full-face respirators.

Working there was an absolute chit chow. It was a dirty warehouse full of dirty, perverted men who all had it out for each other. They would steal from each other's desks and eat each other's food in the fridge, even if it had their name on it. People would go outside to their cars and drink hard liquor and come back inside to operate heavy machinery. Employees would start rumors about you, then look at your butt when you walked past them out on the floor. I tried to keep it modest, wearing T-shirts and black leggings, but my boss knew what was happening and would parade around the plant in sundresses. While she liked the attention, I wanted to crawl into a hole.

Being around my boss made me feel physically ill. I had to sit through stories and pretend I cared about her toddler throwing temper tantrums because they only wanted the marshmallows out of the cereal. Then I had to hear all the stories about how the maintenance man was "harassing" her, and she, supposedly, wanted nothing to do with it. Meanwhile, she was having an affair with him while wearing a five-year anniversary rock on her finger that her husband had just bought her, teaching me the golden rule of the workplace: don't chit where you eat. She talked openly about everyone else's business, including how much money the employees made and how they were all jealous of her because she made more. She changed a lot of rules and implemented a lot of new procedures—some for the better, some simply because she had the power to do so. She fired everyone who got in her way, eventually including me.

Other employees cut corners and did not follow industrial protocol. They believed they would make more money producing rubber belts on broken machines rather than shutting them down to repair them because they would lose money during downtime. They wound up losing more money because all belts produced on broken equipment were out of spec, and they had to get rid of them and shut down the machines anyway.

Other employees stole scrap metal to sell it, stole cleaning supplies out of the closets to bring home to their families, and someone even stole the power washer. When I tried looking at the cameras, I couldn't catch them. People would pee in a room with abandoned machinery instead of walking fifty feet to the bathroom. Old men would stare at me through the window of my office door and would not leave until I looked up and acknowledged them. Instead of my boss firing that one, I got a cubicle installed for me to hide behind in the middle of an open office.

The infrastructure of that place was a joke. People's offices would flood when we tested the fire hydrants during safety audits. Pieces of equipment would spontaneously combust out on the plant floor, and the iron beams designed to support multiple rubber belts, each weighing over a ton, were bent from forklifts banging into them. The foundation of the plant was crumbling, and the company spent hundreds of thousands of dollars on Band-Aids instead of just shutting it the fug down.

Apparently, I wasn't the only one who wanted it to shut down because during one of my safety inspections, I found at least twenty cigarette butts thrown on top of papers inside of the boiler room, the most flammable room in the building. And of course, that was the only place in the plant that wasn't on camera.

The industry had its claws deep in me. Refusing to use my powers for evil and work for the oil industry, I settled for where life took me, once again. Unfulfilled and ignoring my intuition, yet again —until the call got so loud that I was forced to make a change.

Cue the over-production of stress hormones my body was familiar with. I was grinding my teeth at night, my body was starting to store adipose tissue, and I would get up in the morning lacking the energy to brush my teeth or hair and not even change out of the clothes I had slept in. I was crying every day while driving to work and thinking about driving off the highway. I would wipe the tears off and go into work with a smile on my face and had to be nice to people who were praying for my downfall. Old men couldn't stand a young lady telling them what to do.

Then, I would cry again on the way home from work, begging for this to be over. I would fantasize about getting sick or breaking a limb so I would not have to go into work for an extended time. I wasn't the only one because we had multiple people faking disabilities and getting paid for it. My energy was completely drained. I was experiencing immense anxiety again and was unable to focus, and as you could see from my thoughts, I was not mentally stable.

I started eating items foreign to my diet like bacon, pasta, and other processed garbage. I binged on junk food due to stress, repeating my detrimental childhood habits. I stopped exercising and continued to drink alcohol as if I was an invincible college student. It was so hard to give my energy to intentionally making healthy decisions when I had to work full-time in a discouraging environment. I barely had the energy to cook myself a decent meal. However, I did stop smoking cigarettes—partially because I didn't feel well, partially because I would get hit on by creepy old men in the smoker's section at work.

I was struggling, trying to carry on with everyday life—getting out of bed at seven AM, stopping to get a sugary coffee, and telling my boss I was stuck in traffic, only to walk in holding a disposable coffee cup, obviously lying. After getting reprimanded for being two minutes late, I would sit at a computer screen for eight-plus hours a day to destroy my body and bone structure, organizing

Excel documents but getting nothing substantial accomplished. I was doing nothing to benefit the planet except for, occasionally, opening an incognito tab to search for a new job. I was trying so desperately to escape the nine-to-five that I found myself in an even worse position—overlooked and underpaid from not knowing my own worth.

I would go home and drink alcohol until I passed out. I would get so sick I would not be able to leave the toilet or hold down sips of water the next day. I would promise myself never to do that again and immediately go for the booze once I felt better. I was getting sicker and sicker, unable to escape a deep fatigue that sleeping all weekend (if I wasn't drinking) wouldn't fix. Not having the energy to ready myself in the morning, I just rolled out of bed and into my car, still crawling through survival mode and up to the coffee drive-through line. I was calling out of work more frequently. You can only use food poisoning as an excuse so many times. You could guess how that ended.

That summer would pan out to be the worst summer of my life. I was working my first nine-to-five job, drinking myself into oblivion, and nullifying all the hard work I had done in college. For some reason, July felt like the longest month we've ever lived. I say "we" because my sister can attest.

Around the end of July, while working, I received a phone call from my mom saying that my sister had passed out from a drug overdose. She had been at the doctor's office, getting a physical before going to college. She had gone into the bathroom, and after not hearing from her for several minutes, the doctors started knocking on the door calling her name. After no response and the door being locked, they forced it open and found her passed out on the floor, turning gray.

I'd had a feeling she was up to something shady but had no idea it had progressed that far—ignoring my intuition. I knew she was smoking because she would always come home smelling like weed and cigarettes, but never did I think it extended to hard drugs. She was stumbling around like a fool from time to time but had a prescription for benzos and antidepressants, so I figured it was just that.

Until one day, I found a syringe in her room, hidden in a box of tampons. She would never clean her room, so my whole life, I just did it to help her. This was familiar territory, but now I had no idea what to do. I called my two best friends from high school. They told me not to freak out and jump to conclusions without talking to my sister. They told me to go to my parents with this one. That's usually my last resort because I wind up leaving with more problems than before.

My dad was the only other person in the house, so I brought the box to him because there was no way I was touching that thing. He called my sister and told her to get home now. She started practically hyperventilating on the phone, asking, "Why?," texting me asking, "Why? You're making me mad paranoid." I told her Dad needed help with something outside. She came home, and he presented the box, calmly asking her to explain. Immediately, she burst into tears, throwing a fit, screaming her ex-boyfriend had hidden it there to mess with her. I wanted to believe her, but part of me knew she was lying. I didn't want to believe my own flesh and blood would lie to me, so I decided to believe her. She could be very convincing, and that was a bad thing.

Trying to get a straight answer out of her was impossible. She lied about everything and just buried herself in more lies until she couldn't keep track and wound up ratting herself out. She lied about everything between getting a tongue ring to sneaking around, doing drugs. After discovering the syringe, I started to lose trust in my sister and began to put the pieces together.

About a month before her passing out at the doctor's office, we went to see All Time Low in the city. This was one of our favorite bands, so we were hyped. We were running late and heard the band starting to play when we parked the car, so we began running toward the pier. My sister was not able to keep up; she was dragging behind me. She had progressed to not being able to stand up, eyes falling shut, having to go sit down. We almost didn't make it into the show.

After we did, she was sitting down, nodding out in the back of the venue. She said she was just "tired".

My two best friends, (the same ones I called when I found the syringe) even had to rescue her one night while I was away at school. My sister wasn't answering her phone for anybody, so they tracked her location and found her in actual upstate New York. They picked her up and brought her home, all fugged up. They dropped her onto the couch right in front of my parents, and the intervention began. It was clear at this point that something wasn't right, but anytime someone tried to address her about it, she would just lie, get upset and start crying, try to leave and go to the bathroom, or make up some excuse as to what she was doing.

She was always either sick in bed or somewhere out with the car. I was now busy working full-time, Mom was working full-time, and Dad was downstairs making leather motorcycle seats, so nobody kept tabs on her. When she came home intoxicated, occasionally they would yell at her, but other times, they just let her go to her room.

My sister kept finding excuses to not go to school. She would go throw up in the bathroom or say she was anxious or didn't feel well. Mom would make her a doctor appointment, but when it came time to go, my sister found a way out of it. She would say she felt better and Mom would just reschedule it.

My mother was a nurse, but just let her stay in bed all day, so I was confused. If my sister repeatedly said she felt ill, I did not under-stand why she was not dragged out of that bed, thrown into the car, and taken to a doctor to find out what was wrong. Instead, she stayed in bed, whining that she didn't feel well and getting up now and again to throw up. I would ask questions and not get straight answers. I would offer to take her to the doctor, but the appointment would already be rescheduled. Even when she had rescheduled doctor's appointments, my sister would find an excuse to get out of them.

When we finally got her to a doctor, they diagnosed it as her intestines being twisted, which was making her stomach upset. They thought she had this rare disease where your intestines cramped up, and you couldn't digest food properly. They gave her pain meds, which were supposed to just hold her over until her intestines "unraveled". They didn't even know what it was. I bet they made up the name of the disease.

She would wake up every day and start crying alone in her room. It broke my heart to hear, but she wouldn't talk to me. How am I supposed to help her when she won't tell me what's wrong? It's been a problem her whole life; she never opened up or talked to anyone about what was bothering her. We felt bad that she was sad and hurting, but she was not doing anything to remediate the situation and kept everything bottled up inside instead of talking.

When she would try to tell us something, she would break down crying and mutter something along the lines of "I just want to die". How are you supposed to respond to that?

Definitely not by saying "your life's not that bad". Their life may not appear "that bad" to an outsider, but the outsider has no idea what they're going through. This kind of pain comes from beneath the surface, and they don't expose everything because the sense of shame is prominent. Part of their depression or suicidal thoughts may stem from them not opening up because they don't have a secure environment to do so. They need the company of those who will not judge them for what they have done. The past is the past, and it should only be used as a learning tool. Judgments should not be made on past actions. It is when these actions are continuously repeated that a problem forms.

If they do open up, by expressing their pain, even if it's them telling you they want to die, they are giving you the opportunity to help them. They're just a traumatized child crying out for help. They are being vulnerable. The truth is, they don't want to die. They want whatever is killing them inside to die. The beautiful thing about this lifetime is you can be reborn without physically dying.

The second we made any suggestions on things she could do to feel better, she would get defensive and refuse to acknowledge there might be an underlying problem. She would be visibly crying and shaking and just trying to breathe, only saying she was "all good". She would avoid taking any accountability and instead get high and ignore all her problems. At a certain point, I wanted to tell her to "get your chit together," but you can't scorn someone who's crying because it will only make it worse.

She looked awful. She showered and still didn't look any different. I started to connect the dots and suggested maybe she was abusing her prescription pills. I lived through the "Xandemic" in college, when people were mixing insane amounts of benzos with alcohol, so I knew what that looked like. She finally admitted that she was taking the prescriptions for anxiety but was lying about how often, and it turned out she was eating them like candy.

It was clear that she wasn't okay, but she was always out and about, and when she came home, she just went to sleep. When I was with her, it was hard to call her out or even attempt to have a conversation with her. I tried a couple of times, but she would just tell me she didn't feel well, and I would leave her alone—until I had had enough of her chit.

I had told my parents that she wasn't okay and that she was definitely doing more drugs than she let on. It was tough to keep tabs on her because I was away at school and then working full-time; Mom worked three days a week for twelve-hour shifts at a time, commuting to and from NYC, and Dad was outside splitting wood. My parents were in denial and wouldn't listen to me until it was impossible to ignore.

Fast-forward to my sister in the doctor's office bathroom, turning gray.

My mom called me at work and told me she was at the hospital with her, waiting to hear what had happened. I worked the rest of the day and went home. My mom met me at the top of the stairs, distraught, saying, "You were right. It was IV heroin." I remember her words and emotions so clearly.

I went to go see her in the hospital, and I had never seen her so fugged up and lifeless. She didn't look like my sister. She had no color in her face—she was so spun and talking absolute nonsense. I didn't even want to be in the same room as her. After a while, I had to get out of there and just went outside. I was sick to my stomach; I didn't know what to do. I went outside and stood in the sunshine for a while until I called my two best friends and saving graces, who came and picked me up.

My sister called me later that day from the hospital and had the audacity to ask me to buy her a pack of cigarettes—practically begged me on the phone. I told her, "You're in detox; they're not going to let you smoke cigarettes."

"No, it's okay. It's fine. They said you can bring them to me." Manipulating me once again.

"Let me talk to them." I was trying to stick to my intuition.

"They went in the other room. Please bring them—it's fine." She sounded so sad, and all I wanted to do was help her feel better. If buying her a pack of cigarettes was the way to do it, then fine.

This was my first encounter with anything of this nature, so I believed her every word like a fool. I swiped my debit card at the big oil gas station I so strongly despised for a pack of cigarettes after vowing to myself I would never purchase cigarettes again. They did not let her have the cigarettes. I was lied to, and I had enabled.

It turned out the reason she was always getting so sick was from withdrawal. She tried desperately to cover it up and do it on her own, but it was impossible not to notice. You can't blame her for not being able to tell us she was addicted to drugs; she was ashamed. You can't blame our parents either; they were in denial.

I used to clean her room frequently as a child with ease, but this time, it was hard. Still, I had to get through there so my mother wouldn't have to do it. Good thing I did because I found the most obscure things that my mother didn't need to see—paraphernalia, empty bags, more syringes, cigarette butts, pieces of burnt Chore Boy, the list goes on.

She went to rehab and officially got out of our hometown, the place that was dragging her down the most. She had a hard time finding a bed in an inpatient rehab because she was under eighteen, and no place would accept a minor. They didn't want to place young people with older people for fear of influence, even though my sister's experience surpassed many of them. She was placed in a room full of troubled youths with eating disorders and depression, no drug addicts whatsoever. So, she received no help with coping with addiction.

After about a week of detox, she started to look better. Life was breathed back into her; she was self-aware and owned up to what she had done with no shame.

She was supposed to start freshman year that fall for nursing. I was going back to grad school for my master's in chemical engineering. She tried to go to school but soon realized that she was not ready and took a medical deferment for fall semester. She moved back to our parents' house and was going to outpatient meetings around our town but claimed she wasn't getting the help she needed. It wasn't long before she was running around with the same people who had gotten her into this mess, repeating past cycles, and exhibiting destructive behavior. She went back to school in the spring semester, but it wasn't long before she dropped out due to abusing drugs. Back to rehab she went.

This time, I had to clean out her dorm room—with my mom. It didn't even compare to cleaning out her room at home. It was a samurai sword to the chest. It took an emotional toll on both of us. I felt bad for my sister because she really was in pain and felt as if she had no one to talk to. I told her I was there if she wanted to talk, but sometimes you can't talk about such personal things with your family, and I get that.

She left New York and went down to rehab in New Jersey. At first, it was a blessing in disguise because we believed her being home and engaging with the same people was the problem. They took good care of her down there, and she enjoyed it at first. She was set on getting clean and was very engaged with all the meetings and doing the necessary work to rehabilitate herself. Every time I spoke to her, she sounded good, very positive about getting clean. She talked to a lot of people who cared about her well-being. She had a lot of support and many opportunities to better herself, and she began to take increasing advantage of them. She had met good people and was in good hands, or so we thought at the time.

I would wake up every morning with anxiety and my sister on my mind, wondering if she was okay, sober, in good company. Mom would constantly sigh—the kind of distressed sigh that makes you turn your head around, so loud it rings your eardrums, a cry for help. When I asked what was wrong, she lied and said, "Nothing." (I wonder where my sister gets it from.) When I tried to pry, she changed the subject, and I didn't dig deeper because I knew I would not be able to get it out of her.

The emotional toll on the victim's family is often overlooked. Family members feel powerless and end up enabling them. The family doesn't know what to do, so they figure they'll give the addict whatever they want because they think they are helping them. The addict completely turns their back on their family and continues to get high because they now have what they need. The choices of an addict will disappoint you, and you will be even more crushed because you just want to love them and see them get better. But they won't unless they want it for themselves. Your words and actions can be insignificant in the mind of an addict.

Mom tried to hide her emotions at first in an attempt to keep this whole catastrophe from the family. Mom cried because she didn't know what to do, so she gave my sister everything she asked for. Mom is passive, so the addict takes advantage. She enabled my sister because she loves her and wants to see her succeed. Little did we know we would be handing her the keys to the door of her downfall.

Dad basically contributed by declaring, "She can never get high again," and stopped giving it any emotion after she didn't listen. Dad cried once, then put in his headphones and watched TV. People cope differently. He gave my sister a book about addiction, but it was up to her to read it.

My parents had no idea what to do, leaving me feeling I had to step up as the third parent and solve this problem. Every suggestion I made, they didn't listen to. When I voiced my opinions, I was silenced. From the beginning, I've stated that my family support system is a bit flawed, and nobody worked as a team. Mom tried to go to family support meetings, I tried to talk to people who had been through this already, and Dad went outside to skin deer in the driveway to make leather.

Holidays grew to be more stressful than joyful. When my sister was home, she didn't want to get out of bed and go to our cousin's house on Christmas. Once we finally got her out of bed, dressed, into the car, and to our cousin's house, she wouldn't want to go inside. My sister started crying; my mom started crying. I comforted Mom to get out of the car and go inside. Dad was already inside, taking chots of whiskey with my family members. I comforted my sister to get out of the car to go inside. When she didn't want to go, and I started to lose my cool and get snippy, my sister cursed me out and got out of the car and started crying. I got out and hugged her because no more yelling will make a positive difference. We stood there and hugged each other until someone else came outside and asked why we weren't in the house yet. Everyone put on a happy face for dinner.

When she was in rehab, I was told to lie and not talk about my sister's situation because you know the family is going to ask how she's doing regardless. For the family parties my sister didn't get to, I was not allowed to say she was in rehab, receiving help. No one was allowed to know. I was the opposite and desperately desired someone to talk to because it was eating away at me like a parasite. I couldn't keep it to myself. I wasn't ashamed—I needed help navigating this. We soon learned that being silent about it was not the answer, and my mother and I both started to open up a bit. What happened had happened, and there was nothing we could do to change it except discipline the way we moved forward.

I had at least three cousins in active rehab and one already dead from an overdose, so what we needed most was the family's prayers and support. Mom spent lots of energy hiding it from Grandma, only to have everything explode right in front of our faces. Grandma was visiting our house for Easter, and my sister collapsed in front of everyone. My mother and I had to drive her to rehab that night. The more you try to cover it up, the harsher it blows up in your face.

Mom began to open up a bit more after that. She was taking proper precautions to handle this emotionally and physically. She began talking to other family members who experienced the same situation. She spent a lot of time researching different rehabs and programs for my sister. She started asking for help instead of saying "I'm fine". I could tell she was beginning to feel better and I was proud of her to for taking the steps to constructively deal with this.

My sister was stuck within the vicious cycle of getting out of rehab, not having a job, having trouble finding one because she didn't have a car, not having a car because she didn't have money, not having money because she didn't have a job, when what was really missing was a sense of purpose. So, Mom bailed her out and bought her a car. We started another vicious cycle of my sister getting a job, getting fired from doing drugs, hanging out with old friends until she crashed a car or overdosed and had to go back to rehab, getting clean, and trying to get a job again. We're not even going to talk about the boyfriends she brought home...

Wash, rinse, repeat, until my mom either chauffeured her to work or bought her another car. I told them not to give her a car and not to let her out of the house, but they did the exact opposite. She totaled at least seven cars, including the family minivan I was to inherit, so now it was personal. My mom was still going to buy her another car because she believed she was better now. I stepped in and threw such a fit over her getting another car that I pissed the whole family off, and no one wanted to talk to me. I tried to stand my ground but lost that fight. She got another car, and it was totaled within a month.

I had put myself on the back burner for quite some time. I put my life on hold and did what everyone around me wanted me to do for a while. Now, I had finally had enough and was losing my mind. I usually look for the positive in a situation, but after so many lost battles, I felt helpless. I had never been so disappointed. I felt absolutely powerless, as if I couldn't do anything except sit back, not enable her, and love her unconditionally. I learned that the hard way by first experiencing the exact opposite.

Watching drugs change someone you love will really fug you up. You live life, every day, wondering whether they're going to die or not. You hate thinking about it, but the thoughts are invasive. *Lucky to be alive* is an understatement. How many more times were we going to have to revive her with opioid reversal agents? How far out were we supposed to extend ourselves for her if she didn't want to get better?

I prayed for her to find peace of mind and heal. I gave her chance after chance because I thought she was doing the work to get better. I was always worried about getting that phone call. Nothing can prepare you for that. Sometimes, it's when you think they're doing well; then, out of nowhere, you get that phone call.

The hardest thing about having a drug addict as a sister was the fact that I couldn't trust her. She would try to manipulate me into giving her what she wanted. She would lie and tell me she needed the car to go to a funeral or work or some other obligation I couldn't say no to. Drugs took over my old sister. She was never the same afterward. It was truly heartbreaking. Isn't blood supposed to be thicker than water? What happens when it's not?

You're supposed to love them unconditionally because they're your family, but what happens when loving them is draining your soul energy? There was a certain level of detachment I formed in preparation for her potentially not being there one day.

You can love someone unconditionally from a distance. You can wish them health, happiness, and healing while asking them to leave you the fug alone. You can wish them peace and move on. You can hold space for them without overextending yourself if they are going to take advantage and deplete you. Sometimes, the best thing you can do is let them fall on their ass and struggle, even if you want to pick up their pieces.

It's a very hard balance to find and maintain. You want to help them because you love them, but you can't because you love them. Sometimes, you must hold back and watch them make the mistakes you tried to warn them about.

My existential, overthinking, analyzing self began to wonder how my sister ended up on this path. Was it her tumultuous childhood? Was it the lack of emotional awareness and empathy, paired with little to no physical affection from a father figure? Was it from hanging out with the wrong crowd? Was it the drugs Big Pharma got her hooked on? Big Pharma tends to do that.

The chemical concoctions made by Big Pharma are mimicked from nature. But corporations can't make money off the free plants that so abundantly grow in nature, so they take the active ingredient from nature that combats disease and make a stronger synthetic replica of it, patent it, and treat your ailments. And they make billions in the process. Before you know it, it's treating (not curing) what's wrong with you despite the side effects, which you're blinded to because you feel a little bit better.

The body heals with natural substances but responds differently to synthetic ones. The body develops an addiction to prescription pills far quicker than our minds can adjust to. People believe that since a doctor prescribes it, it must be okay. Big Pharma's goal is having you hooked on drugs forever to make them money rather than healing your ailments and preventing future diseases.

Big Pharma and the rehabs are BFFs. Rehabs hire recruiters to prey on the addicted, who are desperate for money. Recruiters will tell the addict, "I'll give you three thousand dollars to go to this rehab for a month." The addict agrees, because who wouldn't, and recruiters bill the insurance company through some loophole. Recruiters get paid, and the addict gets paid. What do you think an addict will do as soon as they're out of rehab with that much cash in hand?

Yep, end up right back in rehab—if they don't die first. People aren't even making it to twenty-five anymore. Just as Big Pharma planned. Some addicts aren't always serious about getting clean, but they are serious about making money to buy more drugs, so they stay clean and play by the rules for the thirty days of inpatient rehab. It's happening to our friends and family. It was happening to my own flesh and blood.

There are two types of people: people who think addiction is a disease and those who think addiction is a choice. Maybe it's neither; maybe it's an epidemic of unaddressed emotional trauma that extends way deeper than using drugs. Even if addiction is a disease, diseases can be cured. But Big Pharma doesn't want you cured—they want you sick forever so they can profit from treating (not curing) your disease. Big Pharma is preying on sick people, and they know exactly what they're doing. Even when they've had to pay settlements for their crimes, their money will never be enough to replace the loss we have suffered.

Why do drug addicts hate themselves and make life a living hell for everyone around them? Why do they risk putting their set-for-life, 150K, full-benefit jobs at risk to get high? Is it because Big Pharma said these pills were okay to take? Is it because they're depressed and they actually want to die? Is it to soothe their dysregulated nervous systems? Is it their fear of coping with past trauma? Is it genetics or generational trauma?

Some addicts resent their families because childhood trauma is why they're in pain in the first place, but they are unwilling to shed light as to why. They just bury and suppress their pain, hiding it under substances, until they develop a full-blown addiction and are powerless to stop it. By that point, they are more addicted to numbing out reality instead of trying to change it. When they're high on drugs, they don't have to pay attention to their suppressed emotions. Instead, they chase the euphoric feeling drugs give them.

Some run from their problems. They repeat past patterns and distract themselves with destructive partner after destructive partner. They run from themselves when they need to turn around and run face-first into what they're running from. Sometimes, they don't get better. It's agonizing to mourn their loss while they're still here with you because they are not the person they used to be. Drugs change people.

You are in charge of the way you act, but you're not in control when you're addicted to drugs. We either heal or keep repeating the toxic cycle. You have the power to make the conscious decision of whether you want to heal and be a member of society or live life in and out of treatment. People are willing to help you. How far are you going to string them along?

To get better, you must want to be better and help yourself. You're not only destroying your own life but the lives of those who care about you and the lives of all the addicts succumbing to the same fate. Addiction convinces you you're okay while it's killing you. Addicts, do yourselves a favor and get to the root of your trauma instead of hiding your pain behind substance abuse. If you really want to change, you will get help. The only way out is through.

We're all addicted to something, whether it be the doomscroll on social media, alcohol, sugary coffees, or even working out. We dissociate from reality because we hate it here, but admitting we hate it here may just be one of the first steps to getting better.

What I've taken away from this whole endeavor is that we end up being the strongest during the moments where we feel weakest. You can cry, you can scream, you can even punch holes in the walls (I suggest anger management help if you're doing that), but we must surrender control.

I spent so much time and energy worried about my sister that I was neglecting myself in the process. I was sick with worry and grief and not taking care of myself. Where I was once hopeful, I was now losing it. I wanted to keep fighting, but it was depleting me. I had more hope for saving the world than I did for saving my sister. This is what made me realize that to save the world, we must save ourselves, and those who don't want to save themselves will fall away.

I wish I could tell you she got better. I wish I could tell you she hit rock bottom and encountered the epiphany she needed. I wish this was the happy ending I could talk about. She's been in and out of rehab so many times I have lost count.

We finally accepted that we couldn't do a damn thing to help her because she didn't want to help herself. She's been productive when she's off drugs in inpatient rehab, but when she got out, the trouble started again. She would get a job, which she usually held down for a short time but then went off the deep end and wound up back in rehab. I used to think she would be able to beat this, but she has given up on herself. It's disappointing and truly heartbreaking when people don't want to get better. Maybe in the next lifetime.

I was going back to college for grad school that fall, so at least I would have something else to focus on. I had a tremendous amount of support back at school from my friends—especially from Connor who had experienced this firsthand with his sister. I felt supported and loved and was able to survive grad school.

Chapter 9: ... Think I'll Try the Stronger Stuff

Grad school was like a fifth year of college—same professors, same classmates, and same parties. I had the same bad drinking habits, except even worse to try and quell my sorrows. I started dating a friend from college, so life wasn't all bad.

By the end of the year, I had a bit of a falling out with Connor due to a lack of boundaries and him wanting what I couldn't provide. As previously stated, he was my first lesson in boundaries, and when he started to scare me, I had to distance myself. We remained strong for each other throughout the year but were both going through our own chit with our families and the other sorrows we didn't tell anybody about. We were both self-destructive and needed to do some soul searching; our paths needed to separate. I prayed he made it with his music because the potential was there. I prayed for him, his family, and that his sister stayed off drugs.

When the universe pushes you apart, you don't try to fight it—you go with it. Pushing yourself to try and make it work will only bring you down farther. You cannot try to force things; if you do, you may find yourself in more trouble than before.

Then, by the dance of the divine, I was offered a much better job in research and development at a global food and beverage corporation after graduation. I was all about it; R&D is where the magic happens. Yes, it was for one of the major plastic polluters in the world, producing products I wasn't passionate about consuming, but it was better than where I was, so I accepted it with open arms.

I thought I was placed in that position for a reason. I'd found a way to fight it from the inside, like Mother Goose had taught us. It was a much more welcoming environment and more inspiring than my previous job. I would get there early as opposed to sitting in my car in the parking lot. I made the effort to engage with people instead of hiding behind a cubicle all day.

It was all bright and shiny compared to my last job. I was busy, the day flew by, I was intellectually stimulated, and I enjoyed working in a lab. Everyone was genuinely smart and would go out of their way to help you get situated and show you the ropes, and I was working with familiar friends from college! There were smiles on everyone's faces despite the heavy workload on our shoulders. Working for one of the largest global food and beverage producers was laborious. We worked hard but also played hard. We would work ten-plus-hour days and then go to happy hour and drink and talk chit about corporate culture.

I was given a do-over, a second chance to make it. I was in a better position, with better people, using my brain, and I was excited about it. I knew I couldn't fug it up but was continuing to drink the way I used to. I would still go home and get wasted in the middle of a work week. I was still getting sick and calling out of work. Stubborn me was forced to learn the hard way.

I was going about my Saturday in late September like any other day. I checked my dumbphone to see a missed call from three minutes ago from a dear friend from college. I was delighted yet perplexed to see his name on my phone because he wasn't a frequent caller. I called him back. His voice was low, and his tone was melancholy. He sounded so distant; I remember it so clearly.

"I don't know how to tell you this, but Connor... um... passed away... from a heroin overdose." I don't remember what he said after that.

I was speechless. My partner tried to ask me what happened, but I physically couldn't speak. I went outside and sat down in the sunshine, alone, with a weight so heavy on my chest I couldn't stand up, crying so hard I couldn't catch my breath.

My friend who called had asked me to pass on the news, but I was resistant. I had to drop the news to another friend who had just eaten a handful of psychedelics for a weekend music festival. How was I supposed to do that? I eventually picked up the phone, but it took a long, long time.

After experiencing the havoc heroin had wreaked on each of our families due to the actions of both of our sisters, I couldn't even fathom why he would pick up that drug. He even wrote a song called "When Heroin Hits Home" about his family's experience. It will forever remain a mystery to me why he went down that path. This news had come out of the blue to me, but supposedly, he had been abusing drugs for the past year, and I had no idea.

I went through all the emotions. I couldn't stop thinking about him and his family and the heartbreak they were experiencing. I just kept getting sadder and sadder. Never had I lost anyone this close to me before. Even with my sister I had not experienced this level of grief. It shook my fugging world. I started thinking, *What could I have done to prevent this?* I regretted not talking to him for the past year. I wished I could go back in time and message him occasionally and see how he was doing. Part of me was angry and remorseful; I couldn't bring myself to forgive him for touching that drug.

I prayed for his soul to find peace. I knew he had demons trying to claw their way out of him that brought him so much pain. But I was mad. All the intrusive thoughts bombarded my head. *Fug you for doing heroin when you spent all that time talking against it. Fug you for not reaching out if you needed help. Fug you for making all my favorite songs make me cry.*

Sometimes, not even the kindest, strongest souls can fight addiction. It is more than a disease. It is more than a physical ailment. Addiction is ruthless. It doesn't discriminate—mothers, fathers, sisters, brothers, beautiful blonds with big blue eyes, and your fugging best friends.

I drove two hours to south Jersey and waited another two hours in line to get into the funeral home. I saw his old roommates and old friends from college. Even his grandma remembered me from helping Connor set up her Christmas tree a few years ago, but this was not the circumstance in which any of us wanted a reunion.

I stood in line and introduced myself to his parents. I had met them briefly at graduation, but they didn't remember who I was until they connected the dots because Connor had told them about me and my sister. I couldn't bring myself to say anything to his sister; she knew exactly who I was.

As I looked down at Connor in his coffin, he didn't even look that bad. Some faces are sunken in, others look puffy, but he looked good. He was buried in a dapper suit with a Yankees tie and had a baseball cap in the coffin. Next to him was a huge flower statue of a red guitar from his aunt. What a way to go. My friends and I met up afterward at a local bar. The owner came over and gave his condolences. He knew Connor because he had played music there.

Thinking about what he must have been going through put a knot in my stomach. I wish I could have taken away his pain, but I couldn't. I wish I could have been a better friend, but sometimes, what we give is all we have space for. Sometimes, it's the intangible things we give that matter most, like our time, effort, assurance, advice, hugs, and kisses.

I couldn't bring myself to go to the funeral the following day. I was already emotionally taxed and didn't want to take another day off from my new job. Someone at work had asked me what I had done over the weekend, and it took me a minute to formulate a sentence before I started crying and had to leave the room. I hid in the freezer storage room at work and tried not to cry. I tried to hide it from work;

I didn't want the attention, but the harder I tried to hide it, the more painful it was.

Nothing had quite broken me like this. I had lost friends and even family members to drug overdoses before, but nothing shook me like this. This time broke my heart into a million pieces and left me lying in agony on the floor. I was sick with grief and would not eat all day and then binge at night because I was starving—and then get sick after. I was resorting to my old habits, which had me drowning. Every time I thought about it, tears came to my eyes. I couldn't stop crying for weeks straight. I had so many questions.

Seeing your best friends reduced to funeral cards will really fug you up. Seeing them dead in open caskets in front of you will fug you up even more.

I fell into a deep depression after losing Connor. I was grieving harder than I ever had in my life. I was hiding it from the people who were lined up to support me and suffering in silence. Emotional regulation was never my forefront, as you have read. I had no idea how to navigate my emotions. I had no energy and wanted to lie in bed all day, but I couldn't. It was hard to muster the energy to do anything, but you have to do what you can with the energy you're able to exert at that time. Sometimes, you're going to have to force yourself to get out of bed and go to work. Sometimes, you can only bring yourself to brush your teeth that day. We must remember to be gentle with ourselves and celebrate the little wins, even if it's taking a shower or eating lunch.

I started doing things for myself that brought me back to feeling alive (dancing to live music). I got in touch with the things that really mattered to me (socializing with friends and family who are still here). I did things that sparked my creativity (writing). I made a cup of tea, watched a live performance of my favorite band, read my favorite book, watched my favorite movie, drew pictures, and did gentle exercises (stretching and walking). I allowed myself to cry—it was a great way to purge. I allowed myself to deeply feel every emotion I previously tried to subdue. We spend so much time and energy numbing pain when feeling it is the only way through.

I poured my focus into doing a really good job at work. It worked for me at the time. I didn't know how else to grieve. I was holding onto a lot of unprocessed anger and thinking malicious thoughts. I was angry at the way things were and struggled to find forgiveness in my heart.

Grief is a ritual, and we must honor it as such. What saved me was believing that this incessant grief wouldn't last forever. We must engage in it as we need but not get stuck in the negative feedback loop. Cry as hard as you may need to, but focus on moving forward. We slowly get over it, but grief comes in waves. One day, you'll feel fine, and the next, you'll be crying as if it had just happened the day before. It hits us especially hard on anniversaries or birthdays. Grief has no timeline.

We held a celebration in honor of Connor's life at none other than our favorite hole-in-the-wall Irish Pub-Café back near college. It gave all our friends and his family the chance to connect and heal. It was exactly what everyone needed, and I know he wouldn't have wanted anyone organizing it other than his best friends. We ate, drank, shared stories, and played music. We hugged and cried all over each other. It was a profoundly healing experience.

When I was young, my mom taught me if I had something to say to someone but couldn't, I should write them a letter because the words still need to be said. I did just that. I had written him a letter, which I read to the whole bar.

Dear Connor,
On these days where we lay you to rest and grieve through your tragic passing, no one is remembering the bad times—only good. We loved you so hard, Connor. You were our homie. You had our backs, and we had yours. You introduced all of us to many of the current people in our lives, and it's just a shame it stops here. I pray for you every day—that your

soul finds peace, for your family, that this never has to happen again.

My heart breaks for you, your family, your sister, my sister, our friends, and myself. My heart breaks for your friends who had to see you spiral like this, who had to mourn your death before your actual passing.

We continue to celebrate the good times we had with you because we can't sit around and cry forever. All we can do is celebrate the fact that we knew you and that you're up in the sky, jamming with all your favorite dead rock stars, watching over us with a guitar in your hands. Or watching the Rangers and the Yankees.

Your songs will be forever stuck in my head. I will never forget the countless times we spent screaming along to our favorite lyrics while driving on the highway. I would not be who I am today without you. This world won't be the same without you. There will never be another.

Sadie (my guitar) will miss you. I know you'll always be with me through the songs that come out of my headphones.

The universe pulled us apart before your passing to not drag me down with you, and for that I am grateful. Although it does not make your loss sting any less, it makes life here on Earth that much more tasteful. I love you deeply with my whole heart, and we will forever be missing a piece to our puzzle.

Love, Claire

He was truly one of a kind. He had such a beautiful soul yet was kissed by such torture. It was disheartening because we had all witnessed the start of his downward spiral, and there was nothing any of us could do to stop him. Few knew it had progressed this far—he had hidden it from everyone. There were so many people who loved him and wanted to help him and see him succeed, but you can't fight people's demons for them. You can stand by their side while they battle it out and be there to help lift them back up when they fall, but they have to fight their own fights.

We decided that we would continue the tradition of celebrating his life. Going forward, we met every year around his birthday and went to a Yankees game. The first one we went to, a huge eagle flew over us and landed on a post right in front of the section we were sitting in. It stayed there for the whole game. Tell me reincarnation isn't real.

I wish I could tell you that was the end of drug overdoses happening so close to home. It took about six months to crawl out of that hole after losing Connor. Right as I started getting over it, another one of my cousins died from the same fate. It made all the feelings swarm back, and my grief became prominent again. I honored my grief yet again, becoming slightly better at being able to handle it because no one had broken me as bad as Connor. I started getting over my grief again, and not even a year after Connor's passing, I learned that his sister had succumbed to the same fate.

Back to south Jersey I went for a second family funeral.

Part Two
Revive

Chapter 10: Drunk on Petroleum

Dealing with so much grief in such a short period led me to a downward spiral of endless dread and despair. With my lack of emotional awareness and regulation, you can guess how I coped with my pain. I got fugged up and tried to dissociate. I was repeating the same destructive patterns I picked up in childhood, but now I had alcohol. I knew it was only a simple Band-Aid to mask my pain, but I didn't know how else to deal with it. I learned the hard way, again, that the more you try to suppress it, the stronger it's going to backfire in your face.

I shamelessly loved being drunk. Whiskey gave me a warm, fuzzy, and invincible feeling on the inside. The intoxication from bourbon was comparable to the high of a drug. My body shaming disappeared, my anxiety dissipated, and I loved the false sense of confidence it gave me. I was more outgoing and made a bunch of friends in the bathroom I hyped up but have never talked to till this day. Both the social aspect and the dissociative aspect appealed to me, despite knowing most of my uncles were in AA and other family members had become physically dependent on it. Those who had to drink Big Gulps of whiskey before eleven AM to quell the shakes are no longer with us on this Earth, RIP.

I was out of graduate school for about a year now but kept drinking like it was freshman year. I went on to work my first real corporate job but found reasons to hate life even more. Our family dog I had grown up with was sick and dying, my sister was continuing to do drugs, and my teeth were rotting inside of my head. I went through a quarter-life crisis, not knowing what I wanted to do with my life at such a young age. Losing Connor was the cherry on top of one big melting ice cream sundae.

I was trying to stay strong, but your thoughts and actions control you when you're depressed. When you're not depressed, it's easy to think "just be happy." But when you're depressed, you can't pull yourself out of that loop. You want so desperately to silence your intrusive thoughts, but they won't shut up. The crazy, irrational thoughts that would never come true are the ones that consume you. You don't want to believe you're depressed, especially when you appear to others as happy, and people look at you as a light at the end of their tunnel. You can't give them an honest answer when they ask if you're okay.

I buried my sorrows in alcohol and really started to disintegrate. I kept getting sick, over and over again. I spent many mornings riding that white porcelain bus. My hangovers weren't the type that B_{12}, a cup of coffee, and some fried food would cure. I couldn't hold down sips of water or even smoke to calm my nausea. I would be lying in bed, half-conscious, in absolute agony. I was unable to sleep or do anything except crawl to the toilet, hugging it in misery. Each time, I promised God I would never drink again if he took away the pain, and each time I was lying. As soon as I felt better, I wanted to drink again. I was disgusted with myself and had no idea why this was happening and felt powerless to stop it.

Drinking in moderation is a scam. There was nothing moderate about the way that I drank. It may be legal and easily accessible, but it's also poison. For me, taking one chot progressed to blacking out—

quickly. I knew I had a problem when I would order the beer with the highest alcohol content despite the taste. I loved double IPAs, so taste wasn't an issue, neither was cost when I was drunk. I resisted spending fifty dollars on groceries when I was sober, but happily spent double that at the bar.

I was off my ADHD meds now—after five years, my body needed a break—so alcohol was affecting me differently, but I was continuing to drink as if I were on them. I often wondered whether drinking to blackout was equivalent to my sister doing hard drugs.

I got into trouble drinking alcohol and always woke up with major anxiety, wondering what foolery I had committed the night before. I got lost visiting friends in a different state. I blacked out on my birthday and cursed out my dad, releasing all my bottled-up emotions. I left my wallet in an NYC cab, then another wallet in Mexico City. I lost my first job from calling out too much—big shocker there. I was getting into unremitting fights with my partner over my drunk actions, but I had no intention to stop until one night, I hit my rock bottom.

I was never a destructive, mean, nasty drunk. I may have gone on some crazy rants about science or called out of work one too many times. I might have stolen some fake plants, but I never destroyed anything. Until I did.

One night, in a blacked-out state of absolute annihilation, I destroyed my roommate's sentimental property. Now I have had my fair share of drunken regrets like losing something or sleeping with someone who I didn't even know, but that next morning, I woke up ashamed. The whole house hated me. I hated myself. Having to apologize was worse than any "walk of shame" I had taken in my life.

Rock bottom, baby. You hit it once and then never again. Hopefully. I can't speak for all. You're the captain of your own ship. My rock bottom might not be as bad as your rock bottom, but it was rock bottom for me. For a people pleaser like myself, who would do anything to keep the peace, it destroyed me. I will never go back down there.

That was almost the last time I blacked out. I blacked out one more time on St. Patrick's Day a few weeks later, where I was yelling —to a room full of nobody—"Who wants to take an Irish car bomb?" and proceeding to take them by myself in the kitchen. I was sick in bed for two days after that.

I've had softer wake-up calls before this, but this was the universe slapping me in the face, telling me to get my chit together again. You don't have to be in AA meetings to admit that drinking is ruining your life.

My house was a mess, my car was a mess, my purse was a mess, and my mind was a mess. My mental health was affecting my work and home life. I was overstimulated on caffeine and under-stimulated on life. I was operating in survival mode before I even knew what survival mode really was. I was abusing alcohol because it calmed my nerves. I couldn't fugging think, couldn't fugging focus. I was not doing any writing. I couldn't get out of bed in the morning, and I wasn't able to fall asleep at night. I would skip a shower and not brush my teeth, thinking it was fine, showing up looking put together. I was so consumed with the hatred of my current situation, I didn't know what steps to take to change it. I wanted so desperately to reverse the damage and change.

I was paralyzed to make a move when I had the world in the palm of my hand. Chemical engineer fresh out of college? I could go anywhere. But I was overcome with fear because I didn't know what I wanted to do. Anxiety was stemming from not being where I wanted to be in life, even though I didn't know where that was. I was experiencing the deep fatigue of unfulfillment, craving alignment with what was meant for me. I was questioning my existence and did not have guidance for the first time. It was always, "Go to college and get a job." So, now what? Not having a goal is common when your goal for so long was just to survive.

Suffering inspires change. Pain is unavoidable, but it's useful. You lose your chit, you hit rock bottom, then you make the choice to get better or go deeper. You're forced to confront your triggers before you even know they're your triggers.

Sometimes, the inspiration for getting your chit together can be someone else threatening to walk out on you. Sometimes, it takes losing something important, and other times, it happens when you can't stand yourself anymore and finally decide to reach out for help. Real growth happens when you start correcting your own behavior and taking responsibility for your life.

I used to think there was nothing wrong with me until I realized I was distracting myself by trying to drown out my problems with substances, not knowing where to start to remediate them. I used to want to fix everyone else instead of myself, distracting myself from my own pain. I let other people's problems become my problems and gave my power away. Doomscrolling on the dumbphone to dissociate was making everything worse. Remember when people read books? Now, we just doomscroll for an artificial release of dopamine. It's not the substance we're chasing. It's the dopamine, the feeling.

Alcohol influences our decisions. It's poison and affects our judgment. I loved being drunk because it felt like I was emotionally in-tune and not afraid to tell people to fug off. Not only did it impair my mind, but it also impaired my body and soul. I used drinking as a coping mechanism, trying to drown my demons and sorrows. They only got stronger and resurfaced.

We can try to drink away our problems, but they'll still be there when we wake up. They'll hang around until we hit rock bottom and make the decision to get better. The first step to getting your chit together is realizing and admitting that you don't have it together. So many people pretend to hold it all together, acting like they're fine all the time but are suffering worse for it.

I stepped back and finally read all my writing and reminded myself of what I had previously overcome. I knew I would get through it again, but it would take more of me this time. I knew it was going to take me reaching out for external help instead of battling it internally. I needed a complete detox and nourishment of my body, mind, and spirit. I never lost sight of my vision for writing a book because I knew my story would help people, but how was I going to write a self-help book when my life was a fugging mess?

We must not be afraid to ask for help. There are people who love you and care about you and would do anything to see you get better. You're meant to be here for a reason, even if you haven't figured it out yet. Just know that you're worth it. Stick around to see what's in store.

Music found me in divine timing, yet again. I heard a song by Frank Turner called "Get Better". That song gave me the goose-bumps, shot straight into my soul, and rearranged my DNA. I never blacked out again. Alcohol (especially liquor) ruined me and would continue to ruin me if I let it. Drinking would, inevitably, be my downfall—not just impeding my weight loss but further contributing to the decline of my mental health and stability. I started saying no to alcohol because every time I said yes, it was never worth it. Whiskey was my poison that I would not touch again.

After losing my first job from drinking too much, I found a job I cared about and wanted to keep. I knew I had a second chance to get my chit together. I still experienced tidbits of seasonal depression but never lost sight of the desire to get better. I have always been very driven, despite the circumstances life has thrown at me. Even crying in bed in the morning, wondering how I would carry on throughout the day and get to work, life was easier to handle with a clear conscience. I started to embrace the struggle knowing it would, one day, be over. I started to focus on what lessons I could learn from this situation rather than succumbing to the victim mindset.

There are times when you must suffer through it to get stronger— "It's always darkest before the dawn" or whatever cliché quote is circling around. Whenever you're melancholy or anxious, it helps to write a list of things you're grateful for. Practicing gratitude was a fundamental shift that changed my perspective on life. It helps you attract positive experiences that will allow you to grow instead of being stuck in survival mode.

You must fill up your empty cup when your life is spiraling out of control. I wanted to leave the self-loathing, hopelessness, and isolation behind, so I booked a trip and traveled across the country and saw some dear friends for a nice, healthy reset before returning to the existential dread that was my reality. A change of scenery really helped me. I don't know what it is about airports, but as soon as you walk in them, it's like an instant cure for depression. I had been working for so long that there was no end in sight and nothing to look forward to. It was so draining. Even counting down the days until I left brought me joy. I desperately needed a break to recollect myself and my thoughts.

And of course, I had my old faithful—concerts. Dancing and singing always helped restore my vitality. No one ever felt like chit after dancing and singing along to their favorite songs all night (unless they were drinking). Church can help you if you're about that life. Many say concerts and church have a similar feeling because you're there, singing praise in unison for the same reason—healing.

I started down the long path of healing to find my way back home to my authentic self. For some, it can be a lifelong journey. Others step into their power immediately because this is what they're meant to do. We have the potential to leave behind our old, unproductive habits and become new people. May we get our chit together and let our soul guide us instead of our traumas.

Chapter 11: Getting Your Chit Together

Halting my destructive drinking habit was just the first step. It was now time to focus on the other D's in my life: dentist, diet, and dicks. While dicks can refer to certain male genitalia, this is more directed toward the people in our lives who treat us like chit. I realized what a piece of chit I had been and how I attracted chitty circumstances into my life. Chit attracts chit.

Now, I would like to make this abundantly clear: what works for me may not work for you. Everyone's chemistry is different, and there's no single cure-all. Please take what resonates, and *use your discernment*.

Dentist

We'll start small because this is something you can easily conquer, and hopefully, you are already doing it: go to the dentist. Odds are, you've been doing this since you were a child and haven't stopped, so you may skip this part. But for those who have stopped because their parents have stopped making their appointments, because they don't have dental insurance, or because they're scared, if you want to achieve holistic health, start in the mouth. Just like digestion, all health starts in the mouth. It is connected to every part of the body. So many ailments in the body are linked to gum disease and tooth decay.

I didn't go to the dentist for years and neglected my teeth, only to feel the wrath of it later. I didn't think it was a big deal to skip out on the dentist, and I was afraid of pain. After not going for years, turns out my teeth were decaying under previously filled cavities, so they all had to be drilled out and everything had to be redone. I had to do it in three separate trips because they were on three different sides of my mouth. Nitrous was a hundred dollars each visit and not covered by insurance, so no gas for me.

One cavity was so deep I was threatened with a potential root canal. That had me crying in the dentist chair. I had to turn my head-phones up as loud as possible in both ears to drown out the drilling, but it still haunted me. I couldn't hear whether they told me to open wider or to bite down, and I didn't care. I was gripping the sides of the chair for dear life, preparing to feel the pain. Luckily the pain never came because the Novocain worked its magic. I did great until my last visit.

I was pumped up going in there, ready to get this over with. They had to refill three cavities on my lower left side. After a shot of Novo-cain, the dentist started drilling. He finished drilling out the first two, and as he was doing the third, he hit a nerve that the Novocain did not numb. I was met with a sharp pain that extended down into the void. I had never quite felt a pain as intense. It pierced my soul.

My heart started beating rapidly, and I couldn't catch my breath. My body was tense, and my hands were clenched so tightly on the chair I was making indents. I started crying and had another panic attack in the chair. The dentist stopped for a minute and gave me another Novocain shot. After enough time for it to take effect, back into my mouth they went. They hit that same spot, and I felt that same level of pain.

Cue me crying in the chair again. They offered to stop and put on temporary fillings, but I just wanted it over and done with. I tried to do box breathing exercises to calm down and told them to try one more Novocain shot.

They did. No difference.

I didn't know what was happening and why it wasn't working, but by this time, I was hysterically crying in the dentist chair and couldn't calm down. They put three temporary fillings in, wrote me a script for something to calm me down, and I came back in two weeks.

Every fiber of my being dreaded going back, but I knew I had to get this done. Going back, I was an anxious mess but slightly calmer due to the gracious prescription he had written me two weeks prior. I paid, out of pocket, for the gas. They started off with two Novocain shots and did what they had to do. I felt nothing.

This experience shook me to my core. The whole time in that chair, I was promising God that I would take care of my teeth if he took away the pain—and I wasn't lying like when I was puking in the toilet from alcohol poisoning. If I could go back in time, I definitely would not have skipped out on the dentist (or spend the summer smoking weed and falling asleep after eating chocolate peanut butter candies without brushing my teeth).

I got kicked in my ass for not taking care of my teeth. By trying to avoid feeling pain, I was forced to feel it. Facing what we are trying to run from is how we get our chit together. I felt the pain I was so afraid of feeling and survived it. Please learn from my mistakes, and don't take advice from anyone who doesn't take care of their teeth! I started brushing with an electric toothbrush, using a natural toothpaste, and flossing with a water flosser (I despise flossing, even though it's necessary). I avoided drinking anything with a pH of less than 4.5 because that's when tooth enamel starts to erode. Most soft drinks have a pH of 3. You do the math. I haven't had a problem since.

Diet

When I first got hired at my new job, part of my job was taste-testing beverages. Unfortunately, these beverages were full of HFCS and had a pH of 3. After my meltdown in the dentist's chair and waking up with big, white pimples on my face, I soon realized this wasn't for me. Luckily, I worked at a facility with many different teams, creating many different products, so I was able to move around and work on something different.

With my technical background in chemical engineering, I was deemed a favorable fit for product development on the dairy team. They made ready-to-drink beverages containing dairy. It was a very technical role due to the heat treatment processes needed to make these beverages shelf-stable at ambient temperatures. I said yes because I wanted to climb the corporate ladder, make more money, and get health benefits.

Thanks to the over-demanding and exploiting nature of the corporate world, my eyes were peeled wide open to the heinous, cruel, and immoral operation that is industrial animal agriculture. Or should we call it "The Industrial Exploitation of Innocent, Sentient Animals and Their Reproductive Systems"?

I am going to explain the entire process of dairy production, upstream to downstream:

Dairy is so natural that cows have to be artificially inseminated to produce it.

Many are under the impression that cows produce milk without any external factors and need to be consistently milked or it will accumulate. Cows are mammals, just like humans; they only produce milk after they give birth in order to nurse their babies. They must get pregnant and have a baby in order to produce milk.

Because males sometimes hurt the females when they mate in nature, the industry has deemed it more efficient to collect semen from one bull to impregnate multiple heifers (virgin female cows). The bulls are constrained and poked with metal electric prods, shocking them until they ejaculate. The farmer collects the secretion, then heads to the artificial insemination chute. The farmer constrains the heifer so she cannot move. The farmer artificially inseminates her by shoving their entire forearm up the heifer's vagina, holding her cervix in place, while forcefully injecting bull semen with a twenty-something-inch-long needle. They do it during the cow's ovulation cycle, ensuring she gets pregnant.

The cows get pregnant and give birth. And because milk is money, it is all harvested for human consumption, and not a drop is wasted on their calves. The farmer loads the newborn calf onto a tractor and drives it away to be placed in a holding pen. Mothers cry out for their babies in agony, babies cry out for their mothers in agony, and their cries are ignored as the farmer drives away with the calves. The calves are confined into holding pens and fed artificial formula. Female calves will succumb to the same fate as their mothers. Male calves are slaughtered for veal, often being starved so their meat is more tender. Yum.

The milk taken from the mothers is sent to the processing plant. It can be separated into heavy cream and skim milk using high-speed centrifuges. These components are mixed back together in different ratios in order to claim one percent, two percent, skim, or full fat. It is then homogenized to break down the fat globules into tiny pieces, suspending them throughout the liquid, creating a homogeneous mixture. It is then pasteurized, or it can grow bacteria that can kill you. Then it is bottled and sent to the store for humans to consume.

This process is repeated during the female's next ovulation cycle, not giving her body enough time to recover from the traumatic experience she just endured. Mother cows commonly suffer from mastitis (inflammation of the udder due to infection) due to filthy living conditions. This can cause pus and blood to leak into her milk. Industrial standards allow millions of pus cells to be present in one liter of beverage before being considered unfit to drink.

Cows have a normal lifespan of about twenty-five years but are dropping at only five. Once they fall because their bodies cannot endure any more stress, they are carried away by backhoes and sent to the slaughterhouse for cheap beef. Downed animals, the ones so sick they can't even stand up, are slaughtered for cheap food. If you are consuming their diseased flesh and fluids, what do you think is going to happen?

As a chemical engineer, one of the fundamental laws I learned is, "Energy is conserved. It can neither be created or destroyed, only transferred." Thinking about the life each cow endures, all the pain and suffering wound into their DNA by the enslavement and maltreatment bestowed upon them by humans, only to be consumed by humans, makes me wonder: Why are we all sick and suffering? Mentally, physically, and spiritually? They weren't lying when they said, "You are what you eat."

To feed the world on an industrial level, all empathy, morals, and concerns for animal welfare go right out the window for capital gain. Some butchers cut tumors and cysts right out of the meat because there's way too much meat left on their bodies to waste the whole thing. If the meat has a tumor, the meat is tainted, not just the tumor. Sometimes, these tumors are even included and ground right up alongside the rest of the animal flesh. The animal flesh is already turning brown because it's dead and rotting, so they pump it full of carbon monoxide to halt enzymes from further decomposing the meat.

Carbon monoxide isn't the only chemical used in animal agriculture; carbon dioxide is also used. Because animals must be slaughtered "humanely," they are placed in gas chambers (the industry calls them gas stunning systems) and suffocated to death with CO_2. There are reasons slaughterhouse workers are not allowed to bring their phones into work.

How are these immoral practices able to take place? On such a highly industrialized level? Undisclosed to the public? We turn a blind eye to it because it's on the other side of the production line. There's nothing humane about shoving your whole forearm up an animal's private parts to forcefully impregnate them against their will. There's nothing humane about gassing them to death. There's nothing humane about breeding billions of animals into existence just to take their innocent lives.

You can't fight the farmers; they're only doing their job. They're not paying attention to the immoral practices they are engaging in because they're trying to feed their families. We need the farmers, yes. But do we really need milk?

BUT CHEESE ...

Cheese is nothing more than concentrated casein (protein found in milk) mixed with rennet. Some cheese can't even legally be called cheese because it doesn't meet the standard of identity to define it as such and must appear on the label as "cheese-product". Rennet is an enzyme that comes from the stomach lining of baby calves and is used to coagulate the protein to make it hard. And yes, baby calves have to be killed for it, so not all cheese is vegetarian. Great news now is that rennet can be derived from plant-based sources, making it suitable for vegans and vegetarians.

The milk of a mother cow contains hormones that help her bond with her baby while nursing. Digestion of casein converts it into caso-morphins. Casomorphins attach to the same receptors in the brain as opioids and mimic the effects opioids have on the brain. The high concentration of casein present in cheese causes a flood of dopamine to be released when you consume it, causing you to feel good—just like you would on drugs. So many people openly admit they're addicted to cheese and can't live without it.

Keep in mind, we are a fraction of the size of a cow. Their milk has the biological blueprint to nourish a baby calf to have them grow into a thousand-pound cow (if they're not slaughtered first). What do you think it's doing to us if we're not baby cows?

We don't know any better. We've been spoon-fed information from Big Media about how dairy is good for us and how we need three servings a day. We forget that they advertised cigarettes during pregnancy, asbestos, metal fillings, Teflon, OxyContin, and even put cocaine in the cola.

Our over-consumption of saturated animal fat is clouding our intelligence. Cheese sticks are normalized, quarter-pound bacon cheeseburgers are normalized, the BECSPK is normalized.

Chef's kiss

We must pay attention to how we feel after consuming these products. How many of us willingly consume dairy even though we know it's going to give us the chits later? Why do we do this to ourselves? For sensory pleasure? You're not in control if that's the answer. If you can control what you consume, you can control anything.

We forget the power we possess on an individual level, the power to change the course and dynamic of history. You can't control what's happening on the news, but you can control what you consume every day. Your diet is more than what you eat. It's everything you consume —what you read, listen to, or have in your social media feed. Make sure it's healthy.

No one talks about the carbon footprint, so we're going to talk about the carbon footprint. While industrial production may be necessary to support a population our size, producers must take accountability for their environmental damage. Cows emit methane gas, which is eighty times more potent than CO_2 at retaining heat. Methane is a major contributor to climate change that nobody is talking about, warming the globe at a more extensive rate than CO_2.

Livestock require an enormous amount of land to raise and consume extensive amounts of food and water. There are certain animals which require more resources than others.

The industry uses Feed Conversion Ratio (FCR) to depict the amount of resources needed to raise livestock. For beef, it's 12.5.

Poultry and fish are 1.5.[1] The higher the number, the more animal feed it requires to produce a volume of meat for human consumption.

Factory-farmed animals are fed a diet of mostly genetically modified corn and soy, which is grown using more than half of the available farmland in the United States. Imagine where we would be as society if we used those resources to feed ourselves, not to feed the food we were eating. Maybe if the land used to grow livestock feed were used to grow suitable food for humans, we wouldn't have as many starving people today. But the industry makes more money this way, so that's not happening.

Tomatoes take 26 gallons of water to produce one pound of product; beef takes about 1800. We frequently consume dollar hamburgers, not knowing the consequences for our bodies or the planet. One burger takes around a thousand gallons of water to produce when you consider all the factors of production. One cow consumes up to thirty gallons of water and fifty pounds of food per day.[2] Dairy cows consume more because they're lactating. Add the water needed to grow the crops for animal feed and the water required to keep them clean because they are living in their own squalor. Factory farms use millions of gallons a day. So instead of taking a shorter shower, you can skip the hamburger and save thousands of gallons more.

The Golden Arches are destroying acre after acre of rainforest to make room to farm livestock for consumption. They are destroying balanced ecosystems at an alarming rate, and there are fewer and fewer trees left to convert CO_2 back into O_2. They can because they have the money—because we support them. (Yes, there are corporate bailouts and subsidies, but the food and beverage industry caters to the consumer at its core.)

---

1. Jagdish. "Feed Conversion Ratio Formula in Livestock." AgriFarming. AgriFarming, April 26, 2019. https://www.agrifarming.in/feed-conversion-ratio-formula-in-livestock.
2. Fischer, Hutjens. "How Many Pounds of Feed Does a Cow Eat in a Day?" Dairexnet. Dairy-Cattle, August 16, 2019. https://dairy-cattle.extension.org/how-many-pounds-of-feed-does-a-cow-eat-in-a-day

What became a necessary means of survival for our ancestors has become an everyday occurrence for us, and the world is suffering because of it. Yes, animal agriculture may be more "sustainable" and "humane" on a smaller scale, but what matters right now is that factory scale is happening. Most of the world's meat is factory farmed, and you're most likely consuming it. Most people are eating meat three times a day, with every meal—and sometimes, more than that. With the growing population, the industry cannot keep up with our taste for meat. Our demand for meat is so high that the industry takes drastic measures to supply it. It starts with us. We must change our demand, starting with ourselves, and not support the destruction of our planet.

It's going to get real ugly, real fast if we don't take the time to do some real self-evaluation and change our ways. Even if we stop right now, they will need a certain amount of restoration time. It seems great that fast food is adopting plant-based options until we find out it's all fried in the same oil, also causing alarming rates of inflammation. Maybe the real way to win is to not consume it at all. I don't know about you, but I want to live in a world where there are more farmer's markets and less fast food joints.

Not only do we not pay attention to how we feel after consuming these products, but because the sensory pleasure outweighs other consequences, we are completely ignoring the environmental impact of it. Some don't care about the environment because they "don't have the time" to make changes. They must work full-time to make money to pay rent and bills and feed their families. Everyone is free to make their own choices, and you should do what's best for your own body, but your thoughts and actions must also evolve as you learn new information.

After learning all this, I was not the same; I was shaken to my core. I was disgusted that these practices were allowed to take place, how much people didn't know, and how those who did simply turned a blind eye. I grew to despise the industry I was working for. I wanted to run away and hide, but I still felt like I had to change it from the inside out, so I kept doing what I was doing.

I would leave work covered in droplets of dairy after working (occasionally, crying) at the homogenizer for hours. I was nauseated from the stench that followed me home. I spent many hours working at that homogenizer working with hot, smelly dairy. I became so disgusted with the smell and taste that I made another promise to God: that I would never consume another droplet of dairy if I no longer had to do this. Not lying, like when I was drinking.

I thought maybe I should work for someone else. I applied to a few other places that worked with plant-based plastics and made packaging material out of mushrooms, but no callbacks. I knew I had to get away from this. I knew I had to make a sustainable, tangible change. So, I went vegan.

Cold tofu.

Going vegan quickly reminded me of why I was hesitant in the past to succumb to any societal traditions. Some vegans had an "all-or-nothing" mindset and large spiritual egos, giving off the vibe that if you weren't a vegan, you were a piece of chit. They would hold signs that said: "meat is murder" then verbally slaughter you for eating it. They lost themselves to their emotions and failed to get the point across to those they were trying to educate. While I didn't fully agree on their method of education, I morally aligned with what they stood for. Their passion was there for the right reasons, but they just needed to work on their delivery. Similar to breaking down complex topics while tutoring chemistry, I wanted to help change the narrative so it would finally click with those who didn't understand it.

Vegans are the scientists everyone ignores at the beginning of a science fiction movie. Besides fighting for animal welfare, we're telling you to quell your consumption of animal products because the resources needed to produce them are destroying the planet. Nobody wants to listen because they want to eat steak, bacon, and chicken nuggets, but the problems society is facing are bigger than our personal indulgence.

Going vegan was the first time I felt I could make a tangible difference in the world with my everyday actions. It was the one way I felt like I could break free of corporate control. Corporate wants us to eat this poison-laden garbage full of hormones and sickness, and I would not succumb to their plan. I get it—it can be a hard transition. We grew up eating processed garbage like mass-produced stock lunch meals, hot dogs, bacon, beef jerky, and fast food for almost every meal, so we were addicted to it long ago. It was time to shift my focus to organic, nutrient-dense whole foods and leave this genetically modified, synthetically fortified, inflammatory, processed garbage out of my mouth.

I started doing more and more research into veganism. I learned that these immoral practices against animals extend beyond the food and beverage industry. The fashion industry mutilates animals on an assembly line without pain meds. They force animals to be held down to have their feathers ripped out or their fur ripped off, while they're screaming for dear life, for down feather jackets and boots. Their process has become so highly industrialized, they have quotas to make each hour, so the animals' sentience is completely over-looked. I can't even pluck my eyebrows without screaming, so I would not want to inflict that pain on someone else.

What made the shift easy for me was my sense of empathy. Put yourself in the place of a factory-farmed cow who is repeatedly, force-fully impregnated against her will. We're using the female body as another piece of equipment in the operating process while we should be honoring the female body for being able to produce life. These animals are not machines and should not be treated as such. Billions of pounds of milk are produced, worldwide, each year, with a large fraction of that being dumped down the drain. We forget a living, breathing mammal had to pump that out against her own will. She would rather be feeding her babies, but the dairy farmers took their babies away upon birth and hooked the mothers up to milk machines. No one thanks the cows for providing milk. No one knows what it takes to make cheese or how it's tied to illness and pain.

After going vegan, every vegan goes through an existential crisis as to why everyone else isn't vegan. How do they not get it? How do they not understand? Why aren't others aware of what horrors we are facing? Is it because you don't want to change, and that's what scares you away? Is it because your sensory pleasure is too important, so your ignorance is bliss? Is it a subconscious way to feel superior to something in life? (If that's the case, you need help way beyond what this book will offer.) Is it because you're triggered because we're asking you questions you'd rather ignore? Why are so many people triggered at the thought of veganism? It's the opposition against animal abuse.

As humans have been divided into races, animals have been divided into species. We're willing to invite certain animals into our home to sleep in our beds, but we pay for other animals to be brutally slaughtered for lunch. We can't bring ourselves to look at pictures of animal cruelty but pay for it to take place. We cry when a dog gets hit by a car but we pay for cows to be shot in the head. We cringe when we see cropped ears on a dog but don't bat an eye when pigs get their teeth ripped out and tails docked without any pain medicine. We hate to leave our pets in cages all day but are unaware that sows only know life from the inside of a gestation crate. We cry for the animals locked in captivity yet are paying for tickets to get into the zoo. We're fighting against bullfighting but still pay for them to be hung upside down by a chain, constricted by one ankle, and lined up to have their throats slit. We applaud when the cow escapes the slaughterhouse but still eat hamburgers. Vets are saving animals for breakfast and then eating them for lunch. The same people who are worried about the hormones in soy are consuming the milk of lactating mothers. Make it make sense.

We all possess an innate sense of empathy; we love animals, not just our pets. Cows are like big dogs; both like to run and play, both get scared, both would scream out for their babies if they got ripped away from them right after birth. Both would drop to the ground after five straight years of forced pregnancy and milk exploitation (that's the dairy industry).

How did meat and dairy become convenient? The process for them to come to fruition is anything but. Yes, our ancestors ate meat and dairy, but they ate nutrient-rich meat at a less extensive rate. They consumed milk from cows that were nourished, already fed their babies, and had a little extra milk left over to spare on us humans. Today's factory-farmed meat is filled with trauma and disease, and we're eating it three times a day. Think of the traumatic lives of these factory-farmed animals, being treated as a number instead of a being, eating genetically modified grain instead of grass, all defecating on top of each other, living in their own filth. The quality between then and now has substantially decreased.

Your body regenerates from all foods you eat. As a chemical engineer thinking on an atomic level, I was determined to heal myself on a cellular level. I was going to take control of my health once again, but it was going to be different this time. I was not going to be focused on a number on the scale. Instead, I would focus on full-spectrum nutrition and making sure my body was fully nourished with substances to help me operate at optimal capacity and thrive.

I was not thriving consuming factory-farmed meat and dairy laden with growth hormones, synthetic animal feed, and torture. My face got so puffy and started to break out. My joints hurt and I couldn't muster the energy to work out. I had horrible PMS and an even more painful period. I started focusing on eating a clean, nourishing diet consisting of nutrient-dense whole-foods and supplementing what I was missing. I focused on pairing foods together to ensure I was getting complete proteins (rice and beans, seitan and legumes, and lots of tofu). No more booze and no more bacon. I felt better with each day.

My hormones started to balance without any exterior hormonal influence from animal products. (Even when meat is advertised as "without added hormones", it was a living creature, and its flesh/fluids still contain hormones.) My acne cleared up, I had minimal PMS symptoms for the first time in my life, and I lost weight without even trying. I felt lighter and had more energy. My immune system got stronger, and I rarely got sick. My brain fog decreased exponentially, and I didn't need ADHD medication anymore.

We jump to shove pills down our throats and go under the knife but are resistant to making lifestyle changes. Why do we only change when we need a cure? Why do we not eat for prevention? Processed meat with nitrates is a number-one carcinogen. Big Pharma has pumped livestock full of antibiotics, so antibiotic resistance has become a thing. You thought coronavirus was bad—if we keep this up, there will be pandemics we won't be able to survive. We have become America's petri dish, and we must remedy the situation.

I am here to remind you of the power you hold, even when you may feel powerless. Going vegan was one of the moves I made that gave me a sense of making a difference on an individual level. We have the power to halt and reverse the damage—three opportunities a day, sometimes more, by leaving it off our plates and out of our mouths. We can fight the powers that be, right at home from our kitchens. Consumers believe they hold no power on an individual level, even though change is happening around us as we change our demands. Corporations may have the Earth's future in their grasp, but so does the consumer. The consumer can't sit back and do nothing. Corporations will crumble without your support.

We are moving further and further away from Mother Nature. We must restore our divine balance with her. We're not here solely to make money—we're also here to be one with nature. We forget life comes from the mother, and we must honor and heal her. Right now, she's sick, and we're sick because of our actions. It's time for a new mindset. May we treat every being as a divine being. Times have changed, and our behavior needs to as well. We don't need to continue holiday traditions gathering around dead birds who are bred to be so large their legs break when they try to stand—we can make lentil loaf.

Life is so precious, and it's so taken for granted. We have

completely enslaved sentient life for sensory pleasure. We're exploiting another species' reproductive system for profit and unnecessary consumption. All earthlings matter, and we are treating some as if they don't. What if we were put here to protect the vulnerable? Instead, we are enslaving them, eating them, and wiping out entire populations. We're manipulating their bodies, their DNA, their reproductive systems—playing God with these nefarious acts. And it's all overlooked because... cheese.

We're scared about the world ending and feel powerless to take action, but we have the power to stop it. Best way to preserve the ocean? Leave its inhabitants alone. The ocean produces more oxygen than the trees, especially now because they're all being cut down. Best way to prevent deforestation? Stop eating cheap dollar hamburgers because corporations are funding deforestation to graze cattle.

Every dollar you spend on it funds it further. Every time you purchase it, you are paying someone to slit the throats of billions of animals. You are paying someone else to force-breed them into existence. Again, this is where you hold your power. You can change it by not contributing to it. Even if you can't go fully vegan, just know that with each meal you can make a difference—for the animal, for your body, and for the Earth.

Our ancestors may have had to eat meat and dairy to survive, but we are the ancestors of the future, and we need to change the way we eat to survive now. Human nature is to evolve. People are reluctant to change because they believe they can't make a difference on an individual level, but small, individual steps lead the way to sustainable, long-term change. Small, sustainable changes such as one meal without meat, not purchasing fast food, buying a bidet instead of using toilet paper, picking up one piece of trash, not supporting fast fashion, or using a refillable water bottle will have a bigger impact than you think.

Almond milk and oat milk made their way into the portfolio at work, which was exciting, but I needed a way to release my existential rage while, simultaneously, instilling a sense of empathy on the collective. I wanted to plant seeds in their minds instead of forcing information they didn't want to hear down their throats. I needed a way to educate people without beating them with the ruler (or stuffed deer leg) to force them to learn. This aspiration, combined with my passion for writing, led me to creating a vegan blog as an artistic outlet.

I created blog posts and stickers. I shared recipes that helped me through my transition and, eventually, became staples in my diet. I wanted to show people that it was that easy to follow a vegan diet while also waking them up to the horrors hidden in our everyday lives. It was there if the reader wanted to read it and was an emotional outlet for me. It had a blunt, yet slightly sarcastic, tone. I made sure to own the fact I could be a preachy asshole because I wanted to see the world become a better place—kind of saying, "Wake up, your choices are causing others (and the Earth) to suffer, and if we don't change our ways we're all going to die." I called it Vegan Asshole.

I met some of the largest influencers in the vegan community during the Plant-Based Expo in NYC and presented my stickers and gave them my elevator speech. It was very well-received, they thought it was funny and loved my "eat mushrooms, not animals" design. It gave me confirmation that this was the right move to make.

Healing my body led to healing my mind led to healing my spirit. I continued my healing journey, pulling back more and more layers. As I started to detox my body, my mind shortly followed. I felt better, had more energy, and my brain fog tremendously decreased. I was starting to feel like myself again.

My body and mind were feeling better, but my spirit still wasn't right. I had to address what I was running from, my suppressed emotions and pain. I had spent my whole life sweeping it under the rug, pretending I was happy all the time, until it was eating me away inside. I was avoiding it because, deep down, I knew I had to walk away from the life that was laid out in front of me.

Dicks

Author Neil Strauss said, "If you don't address your childhood traumas, your romantic relationships will."[3] When I heard it, I didn't fully understand it, but I found myself resonating with it regardless.

My partner and I were living a great life. We had our own house, each had a full-time job, could go to any concert we wanted, and had pets. Pets really will distract you from all the emotional turmoil around you. Besides enduring constant yelling, objects being thrown across the room, banging tables, and breaking things, I was living a comfortable life—or so I thought.

Small incidents started to become big problems. Some minuscule mistake I had made, such as measuring something incorrectly or leaving the vacuum in the middle of the walkway, enraged him. Next thing I knew, I was being screamed at, and I didn't know how to respond. I was not a fighter; my instinct was not to yell back. I wanted to run away and crawl into a hole.

This scenario had become a normal occurrence at this point. I would usually just stand there until he cooled off, but this time, I noticed myself dissociating from the situation, just as I had when my father yelled at me as a child. Immediately, that quote made sense, and I was having flashbacks to childhood of being yelled at and running away to cry in my closet. I guess we really do repeat our broken childhood patterns in our adult relationships. Oedipus was wrong on this one because I lost attraction to my partner almost immediately for mimicking my father's behavior.

It was another slap in the face from the big U telling me it was time to recognize this was not functioning, not healthy, and not sustainable. Dissociating can be just as bad as losing your temper. I was repeating the destructive patterns that kept me "safe" in child-

---

3. "11 Unforgettable Quotes from Neil Strauss About Conscious Relationships." Medium. Elephant Journal, September 27, 2023. https://medium.com/mindfullove/11-unforgettable-quotes-from-neil-strauss-about-conscious-relationships

but would not work anymore. I did what I had to do in survival mode, but I wanted to move out of that now. I wanted to change my behavior and move forward to give myself the opportunity to thrive.

I mustered up my courage and said something. It was hard to talk about what was bothering me with my partner because no account- ability was ever taken. The emotional instability of both parties impeded us from discovering the root cause of our problems. No boundaries were put in place from the beginning. I gave up parts of myself in order to be accepted. I was eating foods I was once strict about keeping out of my diet and agreeing to things I didn't want to do based on fear of rejection.

Conversations were deflected once growth was brought up. "This is just the way I am. I don't need to change. I don't need therapy." Once I heard that, I knew this would be yet another battle I would have to fight alone. For someone who desperately wanted to grow and change, I knew I would be held back if I stayed where I was. I knew, deep down, I had to pull back and focus on myself, alone. It was scary to think about, even more painful to admit, but liberating once executed. So, I made the tough decision: severed the tie and got into therapy. Right during double eclipse season (Coincidence? I think not).

Breakups are never easy. It's hard to walk away from something you spent so much time and energy building—even if it's unhealthy, even if you're in love. Loyalty does not mean tolerating pain and disrespect. Recognize the difference, especially if you grew up in a stressful environment. Your nervous system is wired for stress. It's normal to you.

I'm here to help you realize there may be a problem, so that you can do something about it. It's people as brave as myself, who have the courage to step up and say, "I will not take this. I do not deserve this. I know my worth and will not settle," who that will thrive. It was time to pack it up and move on to grander things.

Leaving detrimental environments can be arduous yet tremen- dously liberating. Magical doors open for you once you stand up for yourself and don't settle for less than what you believe you deserve. There are time we lose people, but the love we gain for ourselves as a result is worth every tear shed. Some people are only meant for chapters of our lives, to learn and grow from. When your paths need to separate, let go with grace. It's harsh to realize that you're chasing something not meant for you, but it was time for me to turn around and chase myself back home.

Retreating into solitude was necessary for me. I needed to work through my troubles, insecurities, and traumas on my own, with no outside influence—by myself, for myself. While some may be too narcissistic to even begin to fathom that point of view, just know that by sitting with your own emotions without any external influence, you will be able to establish boundaries and non-negotiables for yourself to ensure you don't get mistreated again in your future relationships.

I knew I had made the right decision but still felt as if I was going crazy, so I sought professional help (and occasionally ran back to my psychedelic laboratory for some research and development). I found a trauma-based therapist and participated in a few hypnosis regression sessions to get to the root of my pain. Both helped me uncover the subconscious pain I was harboring.

When you reach out for help, the people destined to help you will show up, but not unless you give them permission. Open yourself up to receiving this help. While you grant them permission, also grant yourself permission to heal. Allow yourself to go through it.

I learned that events from childhood affect you more than you have the capacity to understand at the time. Growing up, your brain really is like a sponge. The subconscious stores what you learn in childhood, deems it as normal, and uses it to navigate adulthood.

Denial crept in at first, protecting those who hurt me. It took a lot to admit there was a problem. It took a lot to admit I was hurting. No one wants to admit that the people who were supposed to love them unconditionally, take care of them, and protect them, hurt them instead.

For some, childhood is experiencing trauma. Adulthood is dismantling it and not letting it control your life—or worse, ignoring it and passing it on to your children to deal with.

Trauma is more than the events you endured, it's also the imprints left on your nervous system afterward—like experiencing dorsal vagal shutdown, leaving you with an improper response to life-threatening pain. Chronic pain lingers in your neck and shoulders, and you experience extreme fatigue and brain fog. You're unable to properly relax and become hypervigilant of everyone and everything around you, leaving you feeling helpless and irritable.

Learning more and more from my doctor about the effects a dysregulated nervous system has on the body made me start thinking. Was it ADHD preventing me from functioning like a normal human being? Or was it a dysregulated nervous system from living in survival mode my entire life? My nervous system, once ingrained in my DNA to protect me in life-threatening situations, was so overworked from being in survival mode every day. I was exhausted and responding to external stimuli in a dysregulated manner.

If you grew up in chaos, chaos is normal to you. Our nervous systems are wired for it because it's all we've ever known. We subconsciously attract chaos into our lives and believe it to be normal. (What's normal if it's different for everyone?) We are creatures of habit. We settle for mediocrity because it feels safe and familiar to us. We don't fully understand the chaos we were experiencing until we're on the outside looking in.

Things really started to shift for me when I finally admitted I was hurting, when I started shining a light on what I kept trying to subdue, when I took a step back and took accountability for my pain and actions. I was harboring a lot of self-hatred and suffering from it. I came to realize how real the body dysmorphia was and how messed up my eating and drinking patterns were due to my lack of self-love. You don't have to be diagnosed with an eating disorder to recognize you have disordered eating. Once I admitted how much it was bothering me, it was like a weight was lifted, and I was able to start healing from it.

So many of us don't want to admit why we're hurting, or even that we're hurting. We want to stand strong and keep our armor on, when the real strength comes with taking it off and admitting we can't carry on like this. So many of us are living in denial. So many of us resist healing because we believe there's nothing wrong. We can't heal from it if we don't acknowledge there's a problem. It's the only way through.

I decided to pursue this healing journey. Healing on a physical level opened the door to the next level I had to face: healing my repressed emotional trauma. I didn't even know I had repressed emotional trauma because I did such a good job of burying it—until I was cracked wide open like a pistachio.

Now remember, what worked for me may not work for you. Please use your discernment. However, I do suggest seeking professional help to uncover what you may need help with. Taking too much acid and crying might help on a surface level, but we're digging down deep and ripping this chit up by the roots to make sure it never grows back.

After quitting my detrimental habits, I felt I finally had a sense of control over my life again. But my path to healing was only beginning. Which led me to my next question on the never-ending path of self-discovery: Why do we let these people treat us like chit?

Chapter 12: From Parents to Partners

Ancestral trauma will always be passed down. When we're children, our brains are like sponges; we believe what we're told and adopt the behaviors we see. Unfortunately, a lot of us unknowingly adopted traumas that have been running through our family trees for generations.

People either heal their trauma or have children and pass it on to them. Those generational traumas we are unaware of will subconsciously choose partners for us who mimic the same trauma we experienced in childhood, preventing us from choosing partners that will help us deal with our problems constructively.

Society tells us we must get married and have children by a certain age, forcing us to rush into relationships and settle for people who are not right for us. We settle for money and a house when we really want genuine love and compassion. We end up having children and raising them in the same toxic environments we were raised in. Wounded people create wounded relationships, and the trauma is passed on.

Some will observe the chaos around them and realize this is not how it needs to be. This is not how it should be. This is finally the generation to stand up to this unacceptable behavior and change the narrative. We realize we should be operating from a stance of love and empathy, not rage and impatience. We remain conscious of our thoughts and actions to not end up like those who hurt us. It's a tough battle, but we can do it. We have the power to choose which traits of our parents we embody. We have the power to change our habits and the things we don't like about ourselves.

Not believing so is giving away your power. We're strong enough to do the work. We don't want anyone to feel the way we did, and there's power in that. We recognize the toxicity, and we're doing the work to remediate the damage because it ends with us.

Your caregivers may have done the best they could but still have not met your needs. They loved you the only way they knew how with what they were taught. They grew up in the same hostile environment as you. Some adults are walking around with the emotional mindset of a nine-year-old because they never matured past the point of when and how their parents hurt them.

We're not blaming them; we're moving past it. Blaming others is giving away your power. We must realize that everyone is on their own journey and facing their own demons. It's up to us to realize this is unhealthy behavior and want to change it. It is our responsibility to not to let it dictate our lives and adult relationships—because believe me, it will.

We must observe trauma as a spectrum and validate everyone's. Everyone's experienced something traumatic to some degree, whether they're willing to recognize it or not. It's bigger than physical or sexual, black or white. There's mental, relational, emotional, developmental, and the whole rest of the rainbow. This kind of trauma can be hard to recognize due to its intangibility. This is why so many repress it—because it's easy. We believe nothing is wrong because there is no physical evidence, and we can just dissociate from it. This leads us to giving away our power to limiting beliefs about ourselves, about how we may not be good enough, or about how we don't deserve something.

Survive, Revive, and Thrive

Trauma changes your nervous system and the way your brain functions. There are different degrees of trauma, but all have a lasting effect. We will be exploring some of the causes and effects of trauma. It can be induced through many circumstances: insistently being told you're not good enough, having overly strict or critical parents, frequently moving homes, losing people, losing parents, divorce, high conflict in your home, or pressure from parents to achieve certain things by a certain time.

Emotionally unavailable parents make it impossible for you to function as an adult until you take conscious action to heal and reverse the damage. Remember, trauma is more than just "my parents were mean to me". Persistent fears and abusive tactics will have you building walls so far up around you that you don't learn how to function properly because you're stuck in survival mode.

It easily extends from beyond parents, too. It can be from an unsafe place where you grew up or other adult authority figures persistently mistreating you. It's surprising how, what seems to be, the smallest of instances can cause a life of turmoil. Some instances are easily avoidable if we are aware of them.

Trauma can be induced by abandonment in childhood. Some parents abandoned their children and forced them to fend for themselves at a very early age. They were forced into adulthood too quickly and have had childhood stolen from them. People praise children for being old souls. Meanwhile, their internal child is screaming for nourishment and attention because they never got to experience it in childhood. This leads them to lash out for attention in peculiar ways in adulthood, committing atrocious acts while looking for the attention their parents didn't give them.

Abandonment trauma will have them ending relationships before they even start to affirm their fears. Those who were supposed to take care of them failed them, so they believe they can rely on no one. Even if they're in love, even if it's healthy, they think it's a trap because chaos and instability are all they know. Pain and trauma prevent them, as adults, from trusting, making them overthink and shut people out for no good reason except the anxiety in their heads.

Trauma can be induced by caretakers telling their children "everything is fine" all the time. This teaches children to never attune to their emotions. They grow up unaware of how to properly work through them and suffer from alexithymia (inability/difficulty to recognize/express one's emotions). They self-isolate when upset because they were left alone to deal with their emotions as children. When they did show emotions, they were shamed. They now lack attunement in any adult relationships they try to form and attract other emotionally unstable partners (further exhibiting the Law of Attraction).

The Law of Attraction states that what we attract in the physical is determined by our internal vibrational frequency.[1] If we are suppressing our emotions, even subconsciously, we will attract other people into our lives who are doing the same. Those unaware of their trauma will attract others who are unaware of their trauma and, unfortunately, end up unknowingly taking it out on each other and passing it down.

Trauma can be induced by experiencing endless unempathetic violence and rage. Repeated exposure to situations where one does not feel safe will shift the nervous system into a chronic state of fight-or-flight mode, creating illness and ailments in the body. Those in that state adapt to their environment yet also dissociate from it, ignoring these symptoms. It happens so frequently that they unconsciously train the brain to dissociate when tense situations arise, and it becomes the norm.

Further trauma is induced by parents invalidating their children's mental health concerns. Some parents are in denial that their children are mentally ill. They believe their children are perfect and would never need mental health assistance. Some parents belittle the

---

1. "Matching Vibrational Universe." Seek Within You. October 16, 2018. https://www.seekwithinyou.com/blogs/172-matching-vibrational-universe.

child's problems and have the audacity to say, "There's nothing you should be struggling about," or "I'll give you something to worry about." Meanwhile, the child is showing signs of mental illness, and the parents are calling them "lazy".

Trauma can be induced by repeatedly being told:

- "You're not good enough."
- "You can't do that."
- "What's wrong with you?"
- "You're stupid. You will never succeed."
- Or my personal favorite: "You're a chemical engineer— you should know that."

Sometimes, the only things that come out of parents' mouths are what you're doing wrong. They scorn us when we make mistakes and we grow afraid to ask questions. Some micromanage their children as a way of asserting dominance. Those who micromanage will never be satisfied by the work you do.

Trauma robs us of the ability to develop ourselves. It shapes our self-image and self-worth because we believe what we're told from external sources. It can have you thinking everyone is mad at you, and you overthink all your actions even though nothing is wrong. It will turn you into a people-pleaser with no boundaries to protect yourself. It can make you think people hate you because they don't answer your texts (instant gratification is ruining us, but we won't get into that here).

So, we put on a mask and cover ourselves with what we think society or our partners will like and accept. We show them our own fictitious idea of ourselves instead of being our true selves. Being inauthentic might get you what you think you want, but it will not be sustainable long-term.

Parents are unconscious of the damage they're causing because the same damage was done to them, and they perceive it as normal.

They didn't have the awareness or tools to heal from it, so they unconsciously passed it down to us. It manifests in many forms.

Some parents teach their children it's okay to tell little white lies to get out of something, and now their children have trouble establishing any kind of boundary. Some parents didn't pay enough attention to their children, and now their children feel compelled to dominate the topic while others are venting to make it about their own experiences. Some parents constantly berated their children about their weight and destroyed every shred of their self-esteem, leaving them settling for less than they deserve in life because they don't believe in their worth.

Some parents gave their children the "silent treatment" growing up, and their children grew up with absolutely no recognition of how to deal with conflict. Some children felt like they had to earn love in childhood and grew up to embody the savior complex. They get into relationships as an adult believing they can "save" their partner, usually attracting the people who need the most help. They help everyone else and put themselves on the back burner, distracting themselves from their own problems.

Some parents drag their children down as a coping mechanism to deal with the pain they have never processed. Their damaging and hurtful words stick with their children and shape their self-image very early in life.

Hurt people hurt people. Your haters don't hate you; they hate the unhealed parts of themselves you make them see. Miserable people don't like seeing you happy because they're not happy. It triggers them. They're bitter because they don't want to do the work to remediate their damage. They don't want to see you succeed because they're not succeeding. They are not rooting for you. Shine anyway. We will not stoop to their level and match their trash energy. We will remain in our high vibrations to attract what is meant for us.

Some parents were the original bullies, but are you ready for that conversation? They may have fed us, clothed us, and put a roof over our heads, so how could they possibly be the problem? Yes, they provided, they sacrificed, but they paid absolutely no attention to our emotional turmoil. Some parents knew no boundaries—and not much respect either. They will abuse us and demand us to respect them. They are unaware that they are unintentionally projecting their issues due to lack of self-awareness. If you can't help us, at least don't project your own pain onto us. You don't know how badly it's fugging us up.

But not all parents are bad. Some parents are absolute gold and raise their children exhibiting unconditional love, and their children grow up to be angels on Earth. It's usually the parents who are wondering if they're good enough or if they're doing enough, who are the best and are doing more than enough. For some, those questions don't even cross their minds. More and more parents are waking up to their ancestral trauma and doing the work not to pass it down, which is why I fiercely believe we can all get better. It's up to both parties to end this.

We must acknowledge what they did, feel our feelings, but not get stuck there. We must stand in our firmness to move on and heal from it. It's difficult because constant abuse made us so uncomfortable in our own skin that we are portraying behavior we're not aligned with on a soul level. Some numb out the pain with substances, while others cover up their pain with false sarcasm. Some people-please so hard in adulthood they lose themselves. We no longer recognize our worth and settle for less, disregarding our morals and standards. We over-apologize when it's not needed, for things that aren't our fault, to gain approval and love. We don't say no when we want to. We let people yell at us and don't stand up for ourselves. We mask ourselves to the world and are unable to step into our authenticity. We compartmentalize and dissociate from the parts of ourselves we are ashamed of. We bury them deep down and pretend they don't exist.

The body suffers for it. We feel unsafe in our own bodies and ignore, or second-guess, our intuition. We experience extreme tension that never releases its grip, leaving us with knots in our shoulders that never dissipate, no matter how many massages we get. Panic attacks set in, and you cry so hard you can't catch your breath while your chest pounds so hard you convince yourself you're dying. You gain adipose tissue, your eyelids droop, you can't seem to unclench your jaw, you develop a strange hump in between your shoulder blades, you're easily overstimulated, the list goes on. You may be violently hungry but can't bring yourself to make anything to eat, so you reach for the processed junk because that artificial dopamine hits so good.

We power through the stress, repeatedly, until our nervous systems are overstimulated and overloaded to a point where we can't function. We can't feed ourselves something nourishing. We can't get out of bed and go to school or work. We're just existing rather than living. People who are out here "living the dream" are the same ones crying in their cars on their lunch break. They are the same people who believe this is it, that working for someone else is what we're meant to be doing with our lives.

So many of us need to heal our repressed trauma and aren't even aware of it. Many will resist feeling and healing. They refuse to acknowledge their hurt, so they can't even give themselves the chance to heal their pain. Some believe they don't deserve to feel good due to conditioning from past events. They invalidate their own traumas because other people have it worse or their feelings were invalidated when they tried to express them. What you went through happened, and your experience is valid, no matter who believes you. Your own validation outweighs validation anyone else may bring you, and you deserve to let it go and heal from it.

It's hard for them to do so because they have no sense of self-worth because they've lived a lifetime being told who they were and what to do by outside authority figures. They believe they are not worthy of certain experiences due to past voices saying they were not good enough. These past voices are only suffering from their own hurts: rejection, betrayal, injustice, abandonment, the list goes on. They believe their pain is not curable because this is the way it's always been, so this is the way it must be. These are the very beliefs keeping us stuck.

Repressed trauma can lead to all types of ailments, including increased blood pressure, a weakened immune system, autoimmune diseases, weight gain, and reproductive issues, just to name a few. So many aliments are connected to the emotional body. My dad bottled up his emotions his entire life, while holding grudges against anyone who's ever wronged him in life. Where did it leave him? Chronically ill with too many aliments to count. He was in and out of the doctor's office and hospitals my whole life. He was always sick in bed or coughing so hard he sounded like he was choking to death.

Repressed trauma comes out to play in adult relationships in ways such as not being in tune with each other's emotions. We're unable to communicate effectively and end up taking our anger out on our partner, when they have nothing to do with it. We people-please to make ourselves feel needed, most likely for people who don't deserve our magic. We shut down and dissociate when we're yelled at and don't let ourselves feel our natural emotions. We let our pain and anger build up inside of us instead of dealing with it in a constructive way. We don't even have the first idea of how to start unpacking our emotions. Occasionally, we lash out against our friends and family. These are signs that we need deep healing. You lose your temper, you lose your power. When no external factor can make you lose your temper, you experience true inner peace.

My repressed trauma reared its ugly head in all the adult relationships I tried to form. Being shamed as a child for expressing my emotions resulted in me not being able to voice my needs in adulthood. Being body-shamed as a child resulted in an unhealthy adult relationship with food and a dysfunctional self-image with absolutely no recognition of what self-love was. I spent my childhood getting yelled at for not listening and just learned to tune it out because I felt unsafe. I never did the work to heal from my pain or cultivate a safe space, so I carried it with me into adulthood. I just dissociated when I felt unsafe and never did the work to change my patterns.

From suppressing my unhealed wounds, I attracted a partner who was also suppressing their unhealed wounds. We were both unaware of them, taking it out on each other, and unconsciously repeating past patterns. Not thinking clearly, I was acting impulsively from a stance of fear. I avoided conflict at all costs, including healthy conflict, which is necessary. I let unacceptable behavior like raised voices and items being broken go on without reprimand. I accepted recurring apologies with no changed behavior because I wanted to believe in the good in people. I engaged in activities I didn't want to engage in because I couldn't speak up to voice my own needs. I filtered out the parts of myself that I believed wouldn't be accepted.

When I finally mustered the courage to say what was bothering me, somehow, I was the bad guy now. I felt inclined to make them feel better, even after they hurt me. When I tried to say what was bothering me, it was undermined, and I was told "That didn't happen," or "It's all in your head." Meanwhile, it was creeping through my entire body and altering my nervous system, changing the way I reacted to situations and what I deemed acceptable. My body grew tense. I was grinding my teeth again, storing adipose tissue as a form of protection, biting my nails, and unable to focus on anything.

I was coping rather than healing. To cope is to adapt to stress; there is no growth if you're only coping. I was trimming the weeds, not pulling up the roots—treading water, not swimming. We lie to ourselves in order to survive. Many of us refuse to believe there's a problem to begin with. We distract ourselves and pretend nothing is wrong. I did it because Mom did it. Mom did it because Grandma did it. But one day, I woke up and realized my worth and refused to be treated like chit any longer.

For those brave enough to call out abusive behavior, it doesn't matter if they invalidate it and become hostile toward you. It's merely a projection of their own trauma. It's not what went wrong that bothered them, it's the loss of feeling in control. The second you stop taking things personally, your whole life will change. They didn't treat you like chit because you deserved it. They treated you like chit because that's all they've ever known.

Between the booze, bacon, and birth control, I completely lost myself. I gained back all the weight I had worked so hard to lose. I was so mad and felt guilty for being mad. I noticed patterns that were not healthy for me but that I continued to repeat out of fear of rejection. Life was crumbling around me, and I still had to go to work. My head was in the clouds; I was trying to drown out life. I was living on autopilot and letting my past control me.

My subconscious was making decisions, using defense mechanisms I developed in survival mode. Avoidant attachment from ignoring all my problems in childhood mixed with anxious attachment from not getting my emotional needs met in childhood poured over a pool of complete nervous system dysregulation from being in a constant state of fight-or-flight mode all of childhood was a nice cocktail. No wonder my relationships failed.

What I wanted was tranquility because it was what I'd been missing. Instead, I subconsciously attracted anger because it was what I'd been suppressing. I didn't know it at the time, but my former partners were mirroring what I was suppressing in myself.

You don't see red flags when you're blinded by love. Many of us have unconsciously normalized red flags because we grew up in a circus. Now, we're falling in love with major red flags when they show us the slightest bit of attention because we didn't receive it in childhood. We fall for them because they're the first person who called us beautiful when we didn't believe it ourselves. We seek external validation because we didn't get it growing up, yet feel uncomfortable accepting compliments.

I've concluded we're all just traumatized children struggling to live life as adults. We're going to end up exactly like our parents if we don't do anything about it. We may be complete emotional messes, but we're not broken. We are not beyond repair, we just have to clean ourselves up and take off the masks we've been showing to the world.

There is too much madness in the world—we must focus on the

magic. No matter how much time was lost to trauma, there is still time to turn it around. Childhood, for some, is nothing but trauma, and you don't even know it's happening until you're older and plagued with mental health problems. Adulthood is dismantling it and figuring out why you operate the way you do. It's learning your triggers, what triggers your triggers, and what actions to take to constructively deal with them. Have you ever overcome your daddy issues? Nothing can bother you then. But it will forever bother me that "daddy issues" is an insult to women when the daddies caused the issues.

Realizing and admitting there's a problem is the first step to change. Wanting better and believing you deserve it is the second, and taking conscious action is the third.

May we surrender and seek external assistance. Admitting you need help is the start to getting better. Asking for help is a sign of strength. We don't know what to do, so let's stop pretending we do. We're looking for guidance. We're looking for a leader. That's why we're all in therapy, dissociating to social media or spiraling, trying to figure it out. Our caretakers failed us, our partners failed us, and our friends pretend to have it all together but don't have a clue either.

We are ending our own suffering through ownership. Healing requires accountability. You can't heal if you don't admit there's a problem. I don't know who needs to hear this, but being "offended" is avoiding accountability. We are not going to be able to make substantial changes if we do not hold ourselves accountable. If you're easily offended, you are easily manipulated.

The deeper our sense of self-awareness is, the more profound our healing process will be. We must dig deep and ask ourselves why we are the way we are and have the courage to explore the answers. We must let our guards down and accept help to get there. It's easier said than done, but when you look at the bigger picture, it's that simple. You either find an excuse or find a way.

Chapter 13: The Cocoon

Some of us, myself included, need to retreat into solitude in order to take a deep look at ourselves to uncover where we are hurting most without outside influence. I spent my whole life deceiving my intuition, and it led me down a path of people-pleasing, self-hatred, and self-destruction. My healing needed all my energy, and I didn't have anything left to give away to anyone but myself.

I wanted to get better, but trauma runs deep. I wanted to understand the intention behind my actions, why I operate the way I do. So, I moved back into my parents' house (trigger central), but experienced it differently this time.

Two weeks after I moved home, my sister returned home from rehab. My parents went from an empty nest to a full house. Mom was happy; she had both her babies back. Dad was grumpy and had no patience; his nest wasn't empty anymore. I tried to talk to everyone to shed light on where I was hurting. Some hurts were invalidated, others were acknowledged and laughed at; that stung the most. Gathering the courage to say what hurts you only for someone to say, "It's not that bad," or "That never happened," will really fug you up.

Some people never change, and I was quickly reminded why I was so quick to fly away from the nest.

There are people who will intentionally trigger you; it's fugged up. There's something to learn from the ones who trigger us: the ones we despise, the ones we are jealous of, the ones that make us lose our tempers. They trigger us for a reason. Your triggers point to your unhealed pain. Healing doesn't happen when you avoid your triggers —it happens when you work with them. When we're aware of our triggers, they become our teachers. They show us the unhealed parts of ourselves we must work on. They pointed me in the exact direction I needed.

Some won't get better and don't have the desire to. Your healing journey cannot depend on their healing journey. You're going to be waiting a long time, if not a lifetime, for someone else to do their own work. You can't make people change; you can only focus on what you can do. The more you try to change them, the more they resist. You can only inspire them to change themselves by being your raw, authentic, unapologetic self. Some don't believe anything is wrong. Recognize this toxic behavior and release them. But while they choose to stay stagnant, we are growing self-aware of our thoughts, actions, and how they affect ourselves and those around us.

If you can begin to heal in the place you got sick, your energy is unmatched. Now I don't condone returning to the environment where your trauma stemmed from if it's an unsafe situation. If you will be harmed, you have to find a new, safe space to go. But if you're able to start to heal in the environment that got you sick, you will be unstoppable. Returning to that environment with a different point of view helped point out exactly where I needed to do the work.

We must remember to be kind to ourselves in the process, as this is new territory we are not familiar with. We must create a safe haven for ourselves, within ourselves, where we can regain our strength and rebuild ourselves according to our new rules, without any outside-influencing energy.

I was able to create a sacred sanctuary for myself, even in the very house I had tried so hard to run away from. Even if you are living with those who caused your trauma, you can establish boundaries that you will not let them cross. After sticking up for myself and raising firm boundaries in the home that had once ruined me, I had space to think without being crowded by other people's overbearing energy. I was able to shed light on why those who hurt me were hurting. I had time to discover things I didn't know about myself.

I used to get anxious being alone because I wouldn't know what to do, but now I cherish my solitude. I learned to enjoy it. Trauma and anxiety hit you hard when you're alone, but doing this work sometimes requires isolation.

I was able to make room for the more important things in life. I was able to read in silence, get my emotions in check, and didn't have to share a bed with anyone but my dog. I became aware of how I was lying to myself and how I was believing the lies I told myself. It can be nice to have someone there to snap you out of your mental spiral, but when it comes down to it, sometimes we need to spiral in order to rewire the way we think. The fascinating thing about the brain is that we can! We can completely reinvent ourselves. We can start over. Anyone who says you can't might not deserve a spot in your life.

I took a long, considerable look at my previous thoughts and actions. I reflected hard on what I had done to become a vibrational match to the victim mentality and attract low-vibrational circumstances, like saying yes instead of saying no when I didn't want to do something, letting people get in my head and make me feel bad about certain situations, letting takers take advantage of my giving nature, how accustomed I was to people-pleasing and, of course, emotional avoidance sat at the top of the list.

I identified what made me uncomfortable, where in my body I was hurting. I sat with it instead of dissociating. I cried in bed a few times and experienced the invigorating act of purging. I started speaking up about how I was feeling instead of burying my emotions. I stopped lying to myself.

You must identify where you're hurting so you can work through it. By pinpointing the exact moment in childhood in which it formed, you can feel through the emotions you suppressed at the time. Those emotions are still stuck inside of you, trying to claw their way out. It was difficult revisiting my traumatic experiences. It was hard to acknowledge my emotions and allow myself to cry over my past, but sometimes it's necessary to come full circle with it in order to let it go.

Healing can make us sad. We're grieving for the past parts of ourselves that deserved better but didn't get to experience it. I experienced grief over the parts of life I had missed out on, grief over the people I had to let go, grief over people I knew that deserved better, and grief over the death of the past versions of myself. It was painful, but it's necessary to allow ourselves to grieve over our past and how far we let ourselves go.

I felt like chit for so long it was the norm to me. I hated myself, my physical appearance, my inability to say no. It was time to start turning the tables toward self-love and exiting survival mode—no more "just getting through the week" only to have to get through the next week. It was time to move out of survival mode and into revival mode and take back my power to change my life for the better. I was no longer settling for mediocrity, it's vital to experience life to the fullest.

Those who strive to be better are rewarded for their efforts. Those who settle for complacency often suffer. The scariest thing I ever did in my life was leave my comfort zone, but it was also the most liberating.

If you're not leaving behind friendships, relationships, jobs, or other situations that are not helping you evolve, you're not doing it right. Anything that sees itself out the door when you start to enforce your boundaries was never meant to stay with you in the first place. Choose this over the company that's keeping you stagnant. The inner peace you will experience is worth everything you will lose in the process. What falls away is simply not meant for you. It's only after you let it go that life starts to gain upward momentum.

May we shift our focus from what we're leaving behind to what we will be gaining, even if it isn't here yet. Let it go, having full faith something better will come along. Let it go to make room for what's coming to arrive. Transition periods are tough to navigate, but that's where the real magic happens.

Whether it be a traumatic experience, a toxic relationship, or a bad habit (or all three), now is the time to transmute it and let it go with love and forgiveness. Use it as a learning experience; learn from it, transmute it, and never let it happen again. We are not holding onto grudges or stagnant energy. We are moving forward in a state of unconditional love. May we release the versions of ourselves we created while in survival mode and switch to a stance of reviving.

We can't do what is easy anymore. We must do what is necessary. Our trauma is not our fault, but the healing is our responsibility. We must collect our fragmented pieces and make ourselves whole again before we can even consider inviting someone else into our lives. We must be honest with ourselves—no more hiding. We must acknowledge our emotions and learn how to manage them. To be human is to feel emotions, and we must give power to those that arise. It's time to work through our own chit, what triggers us and why, by healing the abandonment, codependency, and rejection wounds we've been trying to mask.

We must dig deep and confront the messy parts of ourselves we've been trying to hide and embrace them instead. We won't get any better until we stop lying to ourselves and acknowledge the pain we've been muzzling. We must sit with ourselves and deep-dive into our pain so that we can learn to love ourselves. We must go through the pain to appreciate the pleasure. We must allow ourselves to plummet through the darkness, or we will never see the light. There's no love and light without dark and down.

So many people are swallowing more and more pills to further disconnect themselves from their suppressed pain. I made it abundantly clear to my doctor I did not want to go back on medication. Medication can be a great crutch and help you get over whatever hump you need to, but they are merely a Band-Aid for some of us.

You must rip it off and get raw with yourself if you want to truly heal and move forward. Addressing your traumas, becoming self-aware of your destructive thoughts and patterns, and doing the work to change course from them will allow you to thrive in life.

We must take care of our bodies, minds, and souls instead of dissociating to a safe place inside our head. No more suffering in silence, hoping someone notices. We must change the narrative and show up differently. We must believe in ourselves and what we bring to the table and give ourselves credit for the work we've been doing to reclaim our lives. We must ask for what we need now instead of attaching ourselves to how things used to be.

When abuse is all you're familiar with, it's your norm. Emotional abuse will really fug you up. Trauma has you focused on the bad, and you forget the good times—like when your dad made you a treehouse out of scaffolding or constructed a life-size train out of plastic buckets in the backyard for you to play in, helped you construct a project that won the science fair, or made your sweet sixteen dress. Instead, you only remember him yelling at you, trying to bang your door down, or commenting on your physical appearance.

Trauma disconnects you from yourself and makes you see the world differently, internalizing criticism and judgment. When you get torn down every so often, you just learn more ways to rebuild yourself. After so many years of just accepting what was presented at surface level without any logical reasoning behind it, I was now demanding better. The thought of staying stagnant repulsed me.

They say it takes twenty-one days to build a habit. If you wake up with the same intention every day of wanting to get better, your life will change. Whether you pray, meditate, or just simply direct the flow of energy, you possess the ability to train your brain. It's a muscle. It takes work to train your brain to tune back in after so many years of training it to dissociate. Training my brain to connect back with my body and allowing myself to feel these suppressed emotions required spending time alone without external influence. I worked on my boundaries, eating habits, and did many different somatic exercises to release the trauma and emotions stored in my body.

I began to incorporate somatic exercise to help regulate my nervous system and drop back into my body. Within our central nervous system, we find the sympathetic and parasympathetic nervous systems. When feelings of unsafety arise, the sympathetic nervous system responds by activating your fight-or-flight response. (For many of us exposed to stressful situations for a prolonged period of time, our sympathetic nervous system has been in the driver's seat for a while.) Through somatic exercises, the parasympathetic nervous system is activated, which tells your body you're safe.

There were so many somatic practices that helped me feel better: certain stretches, grounding, EFT tapping, shaking, breathwork, and singing along to karaoke at emo night. Through somatic practice, I released my tense fascia, unclenched my jaw, quelled biting my nails, lowered my tight shoulders, opened my hips, and began to lose adipose tissue.

By slowing down and connecting to my body, I was able to start to heal my relationship with food. I felt so unsafe in my body for such a long time. Body dysmorphia and other unresolved emotional issues led me to making some questionable decisions. I turned to food as an emotional crutch to try and feel safe in my body, only to exacerbate the feelings of unsafety. I would stress-eat at my desk or stand up and eat over the sink. I would surf the TV to put something on just to eat quickly in a few minutes. I started to make myself sit down and let myself be present while I ate foods that nourished my body instead of eating whatever was in the kitchen for the sake of getting it over with. I still couldn't cook a meal or eat in the kitchen if my dad was in there, but it was a start. Your body doesn't forget how they made you feel.

I noticed how my body responded to being around certain people. Your body will tell you if they are meant to be in your company or not. When they're not, you grow tense, you're unable to open up to them, and you're scared to voice your needs. With romantic partners, you have trouble sleeping next to them at night, you don't like the way they smell, you don't kiss them passionately, and are not sexually attracted to them. The list can look different for everyone. It's up to you to make one.

I started paying attention to how my body felt in certain situations. I noticed how my body felt throughout the different phases of my cycle, and allowed myself to rest and eat more during my luteal phase and not feel guilty about it. Instead, I was able to understand what it needed and nourish it to optimal capacity. I needed a disciplined diet where I could be in control of the food I ate, where I wouldn't binge on processed garbage chemically engineered to make me crave more. I was once so bogged down with saturated animal fat, hormone disruptors and artificial processing agents that I couldn't think straight. I had no discipline toward the food choices I made. My body felt hijacked.

I wanted to eat things that nourished my body and made me feel good. Following a plant-based, whole-food diet while focusing on full-spectrum nutrition did that for me. I noticed a difference in my body very quickly after changing my diet. I had more energy and was more cognizant. I was able to eat without feeling stuffed afterwards and my gut health began to balance itself out. Even if I wasn't consuming certain types of foods, I didn't feel restricted. I discovered a newfound sense of creativity in the kitchen making substitutes for meat and dairy out of vegetables and legumes. I found other ways to satisfy what I thought I was missing. I grew to be so much more comfortable around food. There were so many foods I was once resistant to trying (venison, seafood, foie gras), but I would try a vegan version of them. Processed junk I once binged on, I wouldn't dare touch now. I felt disciplined and in control. After learning how to regulate my emotions, I no longer even experienced the urge to binge-eat.

After evolving and leveling up, my goal became to connect my mind, body, and spirit. Can we all agree we're just collectively uncomfortable and celebrate ourselves anyway? Even the Playboy bunnies have body dysmorphia. By admitting how we really feel, we can process it and let it go so we can attract those who celebrate and love our so-called flaws. Those are the ones worth keeping beside us.

Again, what I did may not work for everyone, so do what's best for you. Use your own discernment, your power. Most fail at first because they believe they don't have any.

Chapter 14: Self-Love

There's too much commotion around "survive" and "thrive" in the self-help category, overlooking a vital step in the healing process: revive. There's no thriving without reviving. How do we revive? We dive, face first, into our pain and love ourselves unconditionally through the process. We are born with an innate sense of self-love, even if others try to dismantle it. It's time to move forward with self-love at the top of our to-do lists.

Self-love may be defined differently depending on the individual. For some, it may mean days at the spa getting a much-needed massage. While this can help, it's only scratching the surface. Real self-love is diving deep and acknowledging our discomfort. It's digging and digging until we get to the root cause, then pulling up our self-hatred by the roots instead of just planting flowers around it like we've been doing.

Changing my habits, one by one, I started traveling down the long path of self-love, doing things that brought a sense of pleasure and tranquility to me. I started getting back into my exercise regimen. This time around, I was focused on strength training instead of mindless cardio, which was wrecking my nervous system for the sake of watching the number on the scale decrease. This time, I rarely checked the scale as opposed to checking it after every workout and getting upset if the number fluctuated a fraction of a whole number. I felt my body begin to change and grow stronger, and that was the only confirmation I needed. When you start to exercise and take care of yourself, everything else falls into place. Your mind gets clearer, and the decisions you were once struggling with become abundantly clear. Don't know what to do? Go exercise, and it will come to you.

Besides treating our sacred human vessels with the utmost love and care, self-love can look different for everyone. What else does it look like?

Self-love can look like respecting ourselves and putting ourselves first. We have been conditioned by guilt for so long that we have deprived ourselves of self-love. We can solve the most complex problems for others, but we struggle to make simple decisions for ourselves. We've been putting ourselves on the back burner and paying more attention to others' needs. We're overextending ourselves and filling up our schedules to avoid the things we don't want to think about or deal with. We're abusing substances to numb our feelings. We're giving and giving until we're so depleted that we have no energy left to work out or cook ourselves a decent meal. Instead, we reach for the fast food and poison our body, which leads to a poisoned mind and, eventually, a poisoned soul. There are so many poisoned people walking around, completely unaware, not even realizing what's happening until it's too late.

Self-love can look like learning emotional regulation and letting yourself feel your feelings. Too many of us self-identify with our feelings when we are merely the vessel that feels them. It's part of the human experience to have emotions, and we must honor them. It's impossible to be happy all the time, and we must welcome sadness when it arrives. Where we once ignored our pain, we must now learn to connect to it. We can't just "let it go"—we must work through it before we can let it go. Like water, let your emotions flow through you because if they stay stagnant, they will start to grow bacteria and can manifest in physical ailments (knots in your shoulders, autoimmune conditions, nightmares, etc.).

Men are criticized for having emotions because they have been taught it's weak to show them, when, in reality, it's one of the healthiest releases. Everyone needs to cry, no matter what gender. It's time to relearn our values and no longer extinguish our feelings but use them to our advantage.

Self-love can look like letting your guard down and opening yourself up to accepting help from safe sources. It will carry you much farther in life than trying to do things on your own. The "I don't need anyone" mentality is a trauma response from past abandonment wounds and disappointment.

Self-love can look like nourishing your body with things that make you feel good, and I don't mean abusing substances. I mean doing the things you enjoy without feeling guilt: gardening, playing with pets, making art, listening to music, and following what lights you up inside.

Self-love can look like ensuring you're getting all your vitamins and nutrients. It looks like fueling your body with nutrient-dense foods instead of that processed junk containing pesticides, hormone disruptors, HFCS, gut biome-destroying toxins, preservative salts, and other shelf stabilizers I can't even pronounce (and I took two years of organic chemistry and excelled at it). Self-love also looks like ensuring your gut health is optimal so it is absorbing all of these nutrients. Health is wealth. Diet is so overlooked in the role of chronic illnesses.

Self-love can look like taking care of your mental health. There's no health without mental health. Prioritizing your mental health will help you thrive in life. If you're sad, you need to get to the root of why you're sad. It's time to start addressing our wounds and attachment styles. You're not going to heal if you refuse to acknowledge the problem in the first place. Self-awareness is an important theme in the healing process.

Self-love can look like addressing your nervous system's need for safety. You would not believe how many aliments stem from a dysregulated nervous system. The nervous system is wired for safety. At our very core, we desire to feel safe, but we are unconsciously putting ourselves in dangerous situations because we have grown up with an irrational perception of what safety is. Regulating your nervous system can look different for everybody. For some it's somatic release, breathwork, or other mindful practices. For others it can look like staying away from people who make you physically tense when you're with them because they make you want to put up your guard and protect yourself.

Self-love can look like regulating our hormones. Continuing along the never-ending journey, I learned what a large role hormones play in general well-being. I used to be under the impression that only diet and exercise affect the weight we gain or lose, not realizing the role hormones play. Everything from adrenal, reproductive, to digestive hormones were all out of whack for me, especially after being so stressed and detoxing from birth control.

The star of this show is cortisol ($C_{21}H_{30}O_5$). It is the stress hormone necessary for the body to perform certain functions, but consistent overproduction from enduring stressful situations for an extended period can have adverse effects on the body. The body's nervous system loses its ability to self-regulate. You can end up responding to manageable situations with life-threatening reactions (increased heart rate, muscle tension, impending sense of doom) or have the complete opposite effect and exhibit no response to life-threatening situations.

While adopting a diet consisting of nutrient-dense food, certain supplements, quality sleep, exposure to nature, exercise, and lots of filtered, mineralized water can help, balancing cortisol sometimes requires rearranging your life to avoid situations that constantly spike it. When you are in high-stress environments, you can do certain exercises to calm yourself down, but these don't always work if there's prolonged exposure. Balancing cortisol may include relocating to new environments, removing people from our lives, eliminating certain foods from our diet, addressing our suppressed emotions, and gently exercising if you can.

Self-love looks like saying no and not settling for what's not worthy of our energy. We're loving ourselves enough to tell others, "I do not deserve this. I will not be disrespected by you." We're no longer accepting the unacceptable behavior that we've previously let slide. Those who drain you and pull you down also help you grow; it's all a vital part of the operation. Those you lose from employing boundaries are not meant to continue with you on your journey. We must accept this because it will become more painful trying to hold on.

Self-love looks like practicing gratitude. How about we count our blessings rather than the number on the scale or the digits in our bank account? Practicing gratitude really will change your life. You will realize every negative situation you experience is a lesson and a chance to learn and grow from. Life will get better once we stop constantly craving something else and are grateful for what we have in the present moment.

So many of us are solely thinking about the future or dwelling on the past. Healing happens when we sit in the present moment. We may not be where we want to be, but we forget we're right in the middle of what we used to want. Take a minute to be grateful, and know that you can create again. Your thoughts create your reality, so change in the physical will shortly follow if you do the work to align with it. If you can't find gratitude for the little things, you won't find it for the big things. Just as we would be grateful for the new house or car we just bought, we must be grateful for hot running water, clean clothes, a bed to sleep in, and a destination for the car to drive us to.

Self-love can look like investing in ourselves and holding ourselves accountable, like by sticking to exercising. It may not be a cure-all, but you're not giving yourself a fair chance if you're not doing it. Movement is vital. You don't feel good because you're probably not moving enough and pumping your body full of toxic, processed food, calling it sustenance. Humans will do anything except exercise. Then, they will complain they are ill. Yeah, I get it, some physically can't, some are lazy, and some are stuck in freeze mode, but for those who can, you'd be surprised how good you feel after, and it makes you want to do it again.

Self-love can look like just drinking water or asking yourself, "Have I eaten something nourishing? Am I hydrated? Have I slept?" Self-love can mean only brushing your teeth. Self-love can look like doing only what you have the energy to do. For once, don't focus on the big picture; instead, celebrate the little wins.

We're changing the narrative to loving ourselves enough to stand up for ourselves and give ourselves what we need. We must show up for ourselves before we show up for anyone else. We must establish selfish boundaries to protect our energy. Being selfish gets a bad rep, but the selfish are harder to manipulate. You are often judged and ridiculed for being selfish, but it's nowhere near as detrimental as giving your energy away to those who don't deserve it. It's not selfish to want the best for yourself.

It's time to worry about you and you only. Man-child boyfriend who can't get his chit together? Parents who have the emotional maturity of nine-year-olds? Siblings who are flying off the rails? Too bad for them. Worry about you and you only. Obviously, you have feelings for them and care about them—we know that. But the time has come to get your own chit together instead of paying more attention to everyone else. You can't get anyone else's chit together for them. You can help them pick up the pieces but only after you've put yours together first.

My self-love list: (Again, this is not medical advice, this is simply what made me feel better.)

- Take care of your teeth
- Stop abusing substances
- Limit alcohol consumption and absolutely no liquor
- Clean up your diet
- Stretch on the plexus wheel to avoid back pain

- Somatic exercises to release stored emotions in the body
- Massage gun to help release tight fascia
- Milk Thistle to help the liver combat the years of alcohol abuse
- Castor oil for the external aliments
- Black seed oil for the internal aliments
- A pinch of mineral salt in your water for electrolytes
- Consume live probiotics
- Don't give your energy to those undeserving of you
- Let go of limiting beliefs and any fear surrounding potential outcomes
- Dance to your favorite music
- Give up the doomscroll
- Create a life you love
- Pick up all the fragmented pieces of yourself and make yourself whole again (I will explain next)

Everyone's list will look different—it's up to you to make one. There are countless ways to revive yourself. This is only the tip of the iceberg. After you pour every ounce of your energy into self-love, watch how much less you care about the things not meant for you.

Chapter 15: The Race Back Home to Our Authentic Selves

Picture your life as a track—like the one you were forced to run the mile on in middle school, the one I pretended to be sick in order to avoid.

It's just you, circling around the track as a child, with all your personality aspects intact, before anyone made you feel shame or doubt about who you really are. You are whole. Each lap around the track is a life lesson. When we complete the life lesson, we can leave this track and go run the high school track. After high school comes college or wherever you go next in life.

As you run around this track, enduring life's lessons, you experience situations that make you feel negative emotions, such as guilt and shame. With each instance of embarrassment, you try to detach and bury that piece of yourself you're ashamed of and continue on with life. What you don't know at the time is you must be whole in order to conquer life's lessons and progress onto the next track. But because you tried to detach from these pieces, you are no longer whole. You keep circling the same track, repeating the same destructive patterns.

We identify with the aspects that kept us the safest, those that helped us survive. That's who we showed the world—the independent little kid that thought they didn't need help. We hid the parts that were vulnerable and needed people, the parts that crave nurturing and protection because we didn't receive it. Since we were repeatedly shamed, we have fragmented so many pieces of ourselves that we are not living in the complete truth of who we are, leaving us stuck in life.

You find yourself suffering, unable to give yourself what you need. The more parts of ourselves we fragment, the harder we find it to truly love ourselves. You realize this is unhealthy, but you don't know how to change it. You want to find a new track to walk around, but you can't leave this track because your parts are scattered all over.

You just keep walking round and round the track, repeating the same scenarios, not learning your lessons until, one day, things get so bad that you're forced to make a change because you're fed up with your own circumstances. You want so desperately to move on, but you don't know what to do. You learn that you must pick up and repair the fragments of yourself. You can't move on until you do so.

Luckily, the track is asphalt, so the pieces you tried to bury are just squished into the pavement. But by this time, they are sunburned, dehydrated, and crying out for help. Those parts still exist, even if you don't identify with them, and they are screaming out for your attention and nourishment. They have been sitting there for a while, hurting, in pain, wanting to be picked back up and nursed back to health.

Good news! The track is circular, so you can loop around and collect the pieces you tried to leave behind. You can't leave them behind. They're a part of you; they help make up your authentic self with your own unique blueprint. Trying to hide them will only attract people who are hiding parts of themselves, too.

Healing happens when you make yourself whole again by picking up these pieces and giving them the attention and love they needed when you left them behind. By telling your "little me" that they didn't deserve what they endured and that "adult me" will hug them tight, protect them, and take care of them. We are forgiving and loving these pieces of our past selves because we wouldn't be here without them. Fragmentation was a coping mechanism we learned for survival in childhood, but by trying to protect ourselves from fear and shame, we have only created more fear and shame.

It's time to go pick them all back up, to hug and kiss each one, to coddle each one in your arms and tell them it's going to be okay. By telling them that they did not deserve to be treated like that, just as you needed to hear in childhood when you were dissociating from them, you pick yourself up and put yourself back together.

You travel to the same depths the universe took you to in order to turn pain to wisdom. We're moving forward, creating space for all parts of ourselves to exist. We are loving and accepting all the parts of ourselves, even the ones that contradict each other. We're human, and contradictions are natural.

There is room for both compassion and cruel.
There is no more room to just play it cool.
There is room for both pride and shame,
Room for the wild, room for the tame,
Room for gratitude, room for grief,
No matter what age, no matter what belief.

After picking them up, incorporating them into your life, and making yourself whole again, you can move onto a new track. You can create a new life with new people who will love you in the ways you need. It will cost you your old life, but don't look back. Know that if you have the gallantry to truly let go, you will receive better.

We struggle until we decide we want better for ourselves and make intentional change. Intentional change can look like addressing our own toxic thoughts and behaviors. It's not easy, but we must do it because pushing them away is far more adverse. We must become cognizant of our repressed pain and anger and bring them to the surface. Once we do, we can watch them dissolve, and our destructive patterns will shortly follow.

Your thoughts are where it all starts. Ask yourself, "How do I think, speak, feel, and act to make sure I am never lined up with that again?"

I know everyone has been born onto different tracks, and some may be in better shape than others, but what matters here is your mindset. Some people are dealt a heavier hand to test their will to surrender to the fact that there may be a bigger plan here.

It's time to release our egos and surrender to the divine orchestration. We must find the balance between finding our power and surrendering what we can't handle. No matter where we came from, we all have a dormant, innate sense of power we must tap back into to take our lives back. Believing you don't have any is the easiest way to give it away.

We are the captain of our own ship. We're releasing past routines and actions we needed in survival mode because they will no longer help us evolve. We are changing the narrative and moving away from the victim mentality. Don't ask, "What's wrong with me?" or "Why doesn't anything good ever happen to me?" or "What if I fail, or what if people judge me?" Instead, ask, "How have I been successful in the past?" and "What can I learn, and how can I benefit from this challenging experience?" and "How might I resolve this?" and "How would my life improve if I committed to changing?"

It's time to redirect our thoughts. Redirecting our thoughts can be as simple as noticing when negative thoughts arise and replacing them with positive ones, becoming aware of when we're overthinking and taking action to reroute ourselves. Deep thought can be beneficial, but recognize the difference between this and relentless overthinking or intrusive thoughts.

Life is a game between you and your intrusive thoughts. Everyone gets intrusive thoughts. It's up to us to discern which thoughts are intrusive and which are relentless. Intrusive thoughts are your worst enemy; they want to tear you down and destroy your self-esteem and everything that you've worked so hard to achieve, similar to the abusive voices from childhood. Relentless thoughts penetrate your consciousness repeatedly so they can be brought to the surface and healed. Once you work though your relentless thoughts, they disappear.

It takes a lot of mental capacity to sit there and consciously pull yourself out of a mental downward spiral. It takes a lot of energy to tell yourself, "I am not doing this again. I am not letting myself go there." But once you get up, move around, and give your body what it needs (food, water, a good stretch, human contact, etc.), you will feel better.

We forget we have the power to do this and believe we are consumed by our thoughts. You're not consumed by anything; nothing controls you. Letting outside influences have control is giving away your power. Realize this, and take it the fug back.

It's bigger than solely our thoughts—to attract better, we must act better. This includes leaving behind all that is not aligned with what we're becoming. Stop returning to what you're trying to heal from. Don't go back to that job—you left for a reason. Don't go back to your ex—you left for a reason. Closure is a joke; you'll never hear what you want to hear. Half of us use it as an excuse to sleep with our ex again. Don't open that can of worms. You need no more closure than the disrespect you're receiving. Not a single soul is worth going back to your old ways for.

Taking conscious action can be difficult. The amount of energy it takes for you to admit and look at your own toxic behavior and do the work to change it can be distressing. The space between awareness and action can feel paralyzing. Don't put too much pressure on yourself to perform right away. This can actually be counterproductive, and we fall back into old patterns quickly because we didn't have enough time to integrate. If we fall back down, we cannot beat ourselves up for it because we are aware of it now. Instead, we are moving forward with a higher level of self-love and self-awareness.

Sometimes, it can take repeating old unhealthy patterns to break the cycle permanently.

Taking action can look like creating something for ourselves, allowing ourselves to focus our energy on something other than working for someone else. It can look like channeling your energy and turning your pain into artwork. People do it everyday through music, paintings, and writing. You grow through the process of creation. It's time to take grounded inspiration and pour our energy into passion projects. You each have your own gifts that the world needs you to contribute. The world needs to hear your voice and see your artistic expression.

I've said it before, and I'll say it again: practicing gratitude will really change your life. It will help rewire your brain to look for the positive in every situation, and not in a toxic positivity kind of way—in a realistic, critical thinking, problem-solving kind of way. Take a minute to slow down and practice gratitude. Write down three (more if you want) things you're grateful for every day, every fugging day, and watch your life begin to transform.

Taking action can look like asking for help when you need it instead of just saying, "I'm fine." Don't be afraid to bother people. Don't be afraid to take up space. Those sent to help you won't run away, no matter how much you think you "bother" them.

No more people-pleasing. It's time to shatter every ego and fear. We're here to make them uncomfortable and speak our unapologetic truths to crumble every lie that exists, no matter who is in the room. We're being louder when we're told to be quiet. We're not looking for validation because we're getting it from ourselves. Saying no is hard, honoring your boundaries is hard, and sticking up for yourself is hard. Suffering is also hard. Choose your hard.

We all possess the innate desire to get better. The body's goal is to heal itself. People are going to rehab, people are going to therapy, and people are committing to the inner work. People are admitting they are hiding from their pain and the fact that they may be suffering from repressed emotional trauma. Instead, may we find ways to incorporate it into our lives and move past it without harboring hate or resentment.

It took tremendous energy, but I forgave those who hurt me, realizing that their actions were nothing more but a projection of their own pain. Wanting revenge left me feeling like chit. I soon came to realize I didn't want revenge; I wanted to get better. It's onerous because they have caused me such pain and inner turmoil, but I tried to focus less on why it happened and more on moving forward without bestowing it upon anyone else. I wished for them to heal.

Some decide to go no-contact with their abusers. Do what you need to do to keep yourself safe. Once given space between you and them, you allow space for healing. It's possible to forgive them and never talk to them again. It's possible to forgive them even if they aren't sorry. It's your choice to forgive them or not, but know that holding onto anger and resentment and harboring pain in your heart is a disservice to your soul. Forgiveness grants you peace of mind.

As we do the work to forgive others, we must compassionately hold space to forgive ourselves as well, for letting us endure situations we would never accept from a healed perspective. Forgive yourself for not giving yourself what you needed and tolerating less than you deserved. We must be soft, accepting, and gentle with the parts of ourselves that we've been battling for so long. We must honor them and be grateful for our past selves, for they endured the pain to get us where we are today.

Forgiveness was in my nature, but moving forward was hard. I tried to have a conversation with those who had hurt me, but I was met with invalidation and stiffness against changing their ways. It got worse quickly. Parents will deny trauma. No one wants to admit they fugged up raising their kid. There was so much animosity held in by those who were older in age, yet emotionally immature. I knew, yet again, that these people would hold me back on my healing journey. I had to do the work to leave once more.

We must take a step back and recognize who deserves our wisdom and attention. To those who don't, wish them healing, and move on with no hate in your heart. We're acknowledging we've been treated like chit. We're not dismissing it, we're not downplaying it, and we're not feeling guilty about it. It doesn't matter if they didn't apologize. It doesn't matter if they're not sorry. They're probably not sorry and don't believe they did anything wrong. You must move on for you. While you're dwelling on the pain they caused you, they're out there living life without you crossing their mind.

Hurting them back will not heal your pain. Louder for the ones who don't listen: hurting them back will *not* heal your pain. Hurt people hurt people, and we are not becoming like the ones who hurt us.

It's time to shed light on your darkness. It helped carry you this far. This chit is not easy. This chit hurts. Don't let the discomfort stop you. Each day is different. Some days, you feel great and as if you can conquer the world. You truly realize the difference between your emotions now and then. You notice and appreciate your growth. Other days, it's sobbing uncontrollably because you're forced to face your fears and childhood traumas.

Sometimes, we need to be open to revisiting a painful experience to discover the root from which our pain stems from. By doing this, we can shine light on the darkness and heal from it. We must let ourselves ease into feeling our emotions and allow ourselves to feel them fully. Laughter is healing, crying is healing, feeling the full spectrum of emotions is healing. Cry if you need to, get angry if you need to, scream into the void if you need to, and then let them pass through. Once you feel them, they don't always hang around.

It takes time to work through our pain, and the process continues through the rest of your life. Be patient and take rest days—your body needs to recover. Not all flowers bloom all year round. Some seasons are meant for retreating and doing the work. Each serves a purpose. Some to grow, some to bloom, others to rest, learn to make room.

You don't have to go through this alone. There's an army of support lined up to help you: people who specialize in mental health, friends who have endured the same struggles, and those watching over you from the astral plane. Do it for every one of your ancestors who struggled to get you where you are today. When you heal yourself, you heal your whole ancestral line. Make them proud.

The universe rewards those who take the leaps. It will give you exactly what you need, exactly when you need it, as soon as you decide you want better for yourself.

After we pull back and focus on ourselves and are operating from a stance of true self-love, we will receive people who are compassionate and considerate with our hearts. Instead of someone who is not willing to meet you halfway, someone else who is will fall gracefully into your arms. You will find someone who is worthy of your time and love, a welcoming environment to be your authentic self. You will know because it will feel right, but only after you regulate your nervous system and can discern the difference between what is right for you and what is wrong.

Just because we may desire it doesn't mean it's right for us. It's a hard lesson to learn. We must establish the balance between fighting for what we think we want and listening to the universe when it tells us no.

We are moving forward with the awareness of whether our current situation is a repeat of our past mistakes or a guide toward a new start. We're leaving behind our karmic relation-chits and welcoming and embracing divine, healthy relationships. We are building a loving home within ourselves and accepting nothing less than someone who accepts and embraces our totality with respect and unconditional love.

We're moving forward with complete self-confidence, with complete surrender and acceptance of ourselves—even the parts we hate. We're no longer watering ourselves down or hiding from ourselves. We're reclaiming our divinity and showing up as gods and goddesses.

We're being patient with ourselves when we slip into our old ways because we now recognize we are slipping into our old ways. We're no longer evading accountability for our actions. We're seeking support when we need it. We're regulating our emotions and setting firm boundaries. We are healing from what hurt us so we don't unconsciously take it out on the ones we live with or the ones sent to help us on the journey.

We're not invalidating anyone else's trauma. We're moving forward, tolerating and validating each other's emotions, and acknowledging the risk it took for someone to be vulnerable. We're being empathetic to how others feel—no matter the age, circumstances, or if we had it worse. They're hurting, and their feelings are valid. It's so important to show support to those who are on the same journey as you, no matter what stage they may be at. When others have worked hard to change, we must hold space for them to show up as that person.

May we exhibit empathy because we were once there, too. May we never judge, for we were once in their shoes. We were once not yet evolved and disillusioned to what we know now. I wonder what we could accomplish if we could recognize we're all on the same team.

We are all on the same team, but everyone is on their own journey. There is no timeline for this. Don't let anyone's age or progress discourage you. Do yourself a favor, and subdue your use of social media. Besides wreaking havoc on our attention spans, it's gotten to a point where we are comparing ourselves to others and feeling bad because we don't have what they have instead of being grateful for what we do have. Comparing your progress based on others' progress will only impede your forward momentum and take away your power.

We're all addicted to doomscrolling social media, so if you're going to use them, you might as well use it to make money and flood your timelines with uplifting and healing messages instead of these rich celebrities with plastic faces who abuse the environment. We have the power of the world at our fingertips with these dumbphones, and we're dissociating on social media. It's time to believe in ourselves instead of seeking validation from external sources.

Survive, Revive, and Thrive

For those who are dealing with the trauma that runs deep in their DNA, for those fighting not to succumb to the same fate, for those who have met their demons while smiling as if they haven't been broken and giving as if they haven't been betrayed, we are phoenixes. No matter how many times we get burned, we will rise up and take back our power.

The ones who are strong enough to admit there's a problem, and even stronger to want to take action to remediate it, will be rewarded for being vulnerable. Once you're on the right track, you will be handed everything you need along the way. You show up halfway, and the universe will meet you with the other half, with all the beauty and abundance it has to offer. The divine delivers, but you must be willing to face your pain head-on and step into alignment to do what you came here to do. Life is a wild ride, but you don't have to do it alone. You will be divinely guided if you open up to it. What they have in store for you is beyond your wildest dreams.

One day, it just kind of gets better (usually after eclipse season, after you've given it all away). When you've committed to healing and are doing the inner work, you wake up one day feeling different. You're no longer facing the existential dread of existence. You're no longer bothered by things that used to trigger you because you've identified them, why they make you hurt, and you've taken action to reverse the damage.

We can't get stuck in self-improvement mode forever. We're striving for progress, not perfection. Yes, we are always improving, but you must pause and applaud yourself for how far you've come instead of worrying about how far you've got to go. There comes a point where you need to stop insistently reading self-help books and make time for integration.

The healing journey never ends. Just when you think you're all good, *boom*. Something comes up you need to work on. As you're doing this, the universe tests you even harder, especially when it's time to level up. Your triggers will slap you right across the face. You can be healing and well-aware of your triggers and still be triggered.

It can be frustrating, but you must take a step back and acknowledge that you're reacting differently to them now. It is in these small moments that we see the most transformation. Something that would once cause you to behave in an emotionally irresponsible way simply doesn't anymore. In situations where I would once get volatile and raise my voice, I found the patience to pull back and let things unfold in front of me. Where I once found myself frustrated over unanswered texts, I no longer checked my phone.

I had lost another dear friend to a drug overdose, right around the time I thought to myself, *Nobody's died of a drug overdose in a while.* Guess I jinxed it. I lost another one of my close friends, a chemE I went to college with and loved with my whole heart. This one broke me just as badly as Connor, but I found myself reacting to it differently this time. I wished him a peaceful transition from the Earth to the astral plane. Instead of being angry he had done drugs, the way I was with Connor, I just kept sending love and wishing him a peaceful passing. I let people at work know instead of hiding in the freezer—I even broke down crying in the middle of a work event. I stepped out of the freezer and allowed myself to grieve the way I needed to and found myself feeling much better this time around.

Trauma doesn't make you stronger. To say your trauma made you stronger is giving it validation and makes it sound advantageous. It's like saying thank you to the fire that burned down your house. Trauma doesn't make you stronger, but it does fug up your body and give you a bunch of unhealthy coping patterns. We cope by making fun of ourselves or using other destructive behaviors to dissociate. I'm all for comic relief, but coping is not healing. It's buying time while you continue to practice your bad habits. You make yourself stronger by deciding to transmute it and not let it take over your life.

It takes work and a tremendous amount of endurance to transmute your toxic habits, but we can do it. We are doing it! In a world that wanted to make me rough and rigid, with raised voices and harsh comments all around, I became so gentle because what I experienced was the exact opposite of what I chose to embody.

Disappearing for a bit to get your life together is okay. We are unlearning everything we thought we knew. We are unlearning fear and bringing back love. From overcoming our traumas to learning to work with our triggers to integrating our experiences, we're honoring ourselves and the hard work it took to endure this journey. Trust that where you are is right where you need to be, but know that it isn't your final destination. Strive to be better, strive for greatness, and put in the work to achieve it. Focus on your inner journey; then, everything will fall into place.

I know you're tired. I know you're lost and looking for a sense of purpose. But you worked so hard to get here. How can you just give up? It's so easy to put something down and start a new hobby. The real test of willpower is the ability to follow through. Breaking your addiction to drugs or binge-eating might not be a test of willpower, but the ability to persevere and finish a task you've started rather than abandoning it is.

Chit happens. Chit is always going to happen. How we respond to it is our test. Let it hurt, let it bleed, let it heal, and then let it go. Nothing feels better than when you experience something that used to trigger you but now no longer holds power over you. This is healing.

There's no textbook for this chit—well, maybe now there is. Even if we don't quite understand it yet, may we go for it anyway because where we're going is better than where we were. Be kind to yourself in the process, pat yourself on the back for going through the things you don't openly discuss, and take time to pour back into your loving cup. The world wants us to be hard and closed off. We must remain open and hopeful. Pain isn't a choice, but suffering is.

The day came when I felt better. I knew deep within every one of my cells that everything was going to be all right. I just didn't give a chit anymore. Others' opinions weren't worth my attention, and I would not let them make me feel inferior. I used "no" as a complete sentence and didn't feel bad. I found myself attracting healthy relationships where I was able to express what I needed, and it was met with helping ears. It was as simple as asking for what I needed and having the willingness to work for it. I was tested hard and had to remain patient while bringing it in. But when it finally arrived, I looked back and appreciated every minute of the struggle.

Focusing on being whole on my own allowed me to effortlessly attract everything meant for me, like a magnet. By focusing on healing my inner wounds and doing the work to change the way I showed up in life, I began to attract more desirable circumstances. I tried new things I was hesitant to try in the past because of what people might have thought. I started listening to new music attuned to a higher vibration because healing was what I needed now. By engaging in events I was actually interested in, by knowing myself and what I would and would not tolerate before entering another relationship, and employing those boundaries, I attracted my divine, loving soul phamily.

I spell this with a "ph" because I met them through listening to the band Phish. Music found me in divine timing yet again. Phish lifted my spirits and give me a new, positive outlook on life. They fully rejuvenated the depleted serotonin in my brain. I lost myself dancing to their music, and it was always a safe space to release my pain. I went from body-slamming people in mosh pits for Fall Out Boy to dancing on the beach in Mexico under the full moon to "Everything's Right". I had an impending sense of doom growing until I heard that song. After hearing that song, it was the first time, in a long time, that I actually believed everything was going to be all right. It helped me change my inner mindset and dialogue to attract situations I was more aligned with. That's the power of music.

Part Three
Thrive

Chapter 16: From Hostile Households to Safe Sanctuaries

I wanted a love that was a safe space to come home to, not one that made me want to sit in my car in the driveway before entering my house—a love where I could breathe deeply instead of holding my breath, where I could speak my mind freely instead of biting my tongue. I wanted unconditional love instead of contingencies, connection instead of attachment. I wanted a relaxed nervous system instead of perpetual knots in my shoulders. No more walking on eggshells—I'm vegan now.

That's the difference between childhood and adulthood. In your youth, you manifest a relationship full of constant sex and answered text messages. In adulthood, you're manifesting things like emotional attunement and a regulated nervous system.

I wanted healthy communication, tranquility, emotional maturity, compassion, consistency, boundaries, safety, dedication to self-improvement, and mutual respect. I wanted to be hugged, kissed with passion, squeezed, and ravished by someone who lit my soul on fire. I wanted vulnerability of the heart and mind while instilling a sense of fun and adventure. I wanted depth, closeness, connection, and trust—

a soulful connection where we could share passion projects with each other.

How are you going to bring in exactly what you want if you don't have the courage to ask for it? By retreating into solitude, doing the inner work, addressing my inner dialogue, changing my thoughts and behaviors, and showing up differently, I got exactly what I wanted.

We attract what we embody, not what we yearn for; desire does not equal embodiment. This is why it's crucial to heal your emotional wounds and start regulating your nervous system, or you will keep attracting the same failed lessons. This is why we must do the work to show up differently in order to attract better, such as detaching from anxious attachment and welcoming secure attachment.

Don't manifest a certain person. It doesn't work like that. You must embody the traits of what you desire in order to attract them in the physical realm. We do this by feeling into our dark side, integrating our shame, and embodying our divine archetype.

Everyone has a balance of divine feminine and divine masculine energy; energy archetypes are not gender-specific. It is when we balance these polarities within ourselves that our divine counterpart will show up in the physical, fully ready to support us in the ways we need. Divine feminine energy is all about surrender and nurturing, while divine masculine energy is more about providing and protection. The feminine comes up with the ideas, and the masculine anchors them into reality. They both need each other to thrive.

The sensitivity and nurturing energy of the divine feminine must be honored. It's sacred. The perseverance and protection of the divine masculine must be honored. It's sacred.

There is an attack on divine masculinity by modern-day society, trying to diminish testosterone by getting men addicted to junk food, porn/masturbation, free short-term sex at the swipe of a finger, ego gratification, excessive amounts of nicotine, and other diminishing habits. Men used to build coliseums and write love letters, and now they cry when they lose their strawberry cheesecake vapes and want to live with their parents forever.

There is also an attack on divine femininity, trying to weaken women by having them operate on the same schedules as the men in society when we have different metabolic rates and hormone cycles and, sometimes, simply cannot keep up.

We are all born with an innate sense of divinity. We are currently suffering because our divine energy has become distorted over time due to outside conditioning, mother/father wounds, or other traumatic events.

Lack of nurturing in childhood has distorted divine masculine energy. Men don't learn how to be good friends, partners, or fathers. He grows up with subconscious wounds and unconsciously projects them onto the divine feminine.

The divine feminine has been hurt by the distorted masculine. She no longer feels safe around him and has lost trust in him. She has guarded her heart and refuses to let him in. She plays the victim and tells herself there are no good men out there. She closes herself off to receiving, pushing herself to operate in her masculine energy, distorting the divine feminine. She is now trying to be the protector and provider, all on her own. Instead of granting her body the rest she needs, she is trying to power through it and ignoring her pain.

Women can operate in their masculine energy and thrive. They can be boss bitches and providers and do just fine; do what's best for you. She may be operating in her masculine energy but may have a partner who is more in their feminine to balance her out (again, not gender-specific—even same-sex couples have a balance of masculine and feminine energy). But it is when she remains guarded and refuses to surrender and accept help that she suffers.

Because the feminine has been operating as her own protector for so long, she finds it nearly impossible to surrender and let her guard down. She gets offended at genuine compliments and would rather open her own doors, even when her hands are full of groceries, even when their man is right behind them. She isn't letting a man take the lead because she wants to feel in control, even when she needs his leadership. She's becoming the man she needs to protect her and is scaring off the men who come into her life who are willing and ready to. She has guarded herself emotionally, mentally, and physically, trying to protect herself from potential love and loss.

If she does let him in, her distorted energy leads her to take advantage of the divine masculine's providing nature for the wrong reasons. She depletes him and then abandons him. This distorts the divine masculine's energy. He is now unable to provide for and protect his divine feminine counterpart, who is ready to nurture and support him in the ways he needs so they may restore the divine balance.

The distorted feminine attracts distorted masculine energy, and the vicious cycle continues. He plays games, tries to control her, he's inconsistent, he leaves her on "read", the list goes on. She chases him because she believes her worth is tied to him.

It is necessary to heal our emotional wounds so we feel comfortable flowing back into our divine archetype, where we can distinguish the safe ones and make room to let them in. There's work to do on both sides, but instead of placing blame on the other side, let us become aware of our wounds and do the work to heal them. Let us show up differently so we can attract different.

Divine men are warriors who want to lead, protect, and provide a safe space for the divine feminine to thrive. It is a top-tier compliment for a man to hear that a woman feels safe in his energy. Their physical and emotional strength is balanced with empathy and compassion. They can be dominant, but never aggressive. They protect us, not control and abuse us.

Divine women are goddesses who want to nurture, heal, express themselves authentically, and support their masculine's vision. Men don't have a clue what women want and most definitely cannot read their minds, so he needs a woman's intuitive guidance and nourishment. She needs his leadership and protection. They are a team, not rivals. To thrive, they must work together. It doesn't matter who's smarter or skinnier or who makes more money. I have a master's degree in engineering and fell in love with a man who had a fraction of the education I did but, somehow, was smarter than anyone else I knew.

Divine men are born to pursue divine women. Ladies, take a step back and let him pursue you. They don't like it when distorted feminine energy chases them. They lose interest if it's too easy. We either overextend ourselves chasing them, or we have our guard up when the right ones come along, and we push them away. We're becoming overly independent and emotionally unavailable when they want us to step back and let them take the lead. But we're afraid because we've been hurt in the past.

Once you surrender and let your guard down for the safe ones, both lives transform for the better. You meet the reason you couldn't settle in the past. You may be blinded to them at first, but they have their eyes on you. You think it's someone else, but it's not, and it turns out to be the best surprise. Something beyond what you could imagine will beautifully unfold in front of you, but only once you believe you deserve it and act accordingly.

Sometimes, we must cut some ties to make room for the new to enter. That urge you get to clean and get rid of everything is new energy trying to enter your life. Sometimes, it's people you need to remove. Leave behind those who drain you and make room for those who are going to replenish you. You usually have to say no to a few of them before the right one shows up. Let go with grace, knowing wholeheartedly that something greater is coming along to take its place.

You may have a certain vision for how your life will pan out, but the universe knows better. You may think you want something or someone, but the universe has a better plan. Don't fight the higher power when they try to take it away. There comes a time when you need to walk away for yourself instead of staying and trying to make them see your worth.

Yes, sometimes retreating into solitude is necessary to heal, but eventually, we must get back out there. Intermission comes to an end, and we must return to the dance floor. Humans are wired for connection, there's only so much healing you can do on your own. We cannot live in solitude forever. We all need people, especially those who have the "I don't need anyone" mentality. You need people more than you think. There are times when we must surrender to those who will help us on our journey. Some people are placed in your life to love you unconditionally, and they come in unconventional, unexpected, yet enticing packages. True love finds you in the process of healing, when it's messy and you find the confidence to be your authentic self.

I met someone through mutual passions (music) and a shared mission (helping humanity and solving the world's problems), and the bond was unshakable. I experienced a deep love shared by soulmates, where they illuminate all your divine characteristics, where they stimulate you intellectually before physically but excel at both. I met someone that provided a safe space, physically and emotionally, for me to flourish. I met someone that motivated me to do better and helped me clean up my act (not in a parenting, up-your-ass kind of way, but in a loving partnership, want-to-see-you-do-better and bring-out-the-best-in-you type of way).

Meeting new people is an invigorating opportunity because you can show up as a new person. You can leave your bad habits behind and feel 100 percent worthy and whole. It was a chance for me to take things slow and build a strong foundation instead of rushing into something for the sake of not being alone. There's something beautiful in taking it slow, even when some triggers arise, because rushing was all I'd ever known. What I now realized was that these triggers were coming up to be purged and released. Even when intense emotions arose, I was grateful to feel everything instead of suppressing it.

I forgot what it was like to feel safe in someone's energy until I met someone with whom I did. It can feel foreign, and you want to run away because it's not the chaos you're used to. Past conditioning can make you think genuine intentions are a threat. Mentally abused people are nonstop apologizing when they have done absolutely nothing wrong. We can't help it; it's been instilled in us our whole lives that our actions were wrong. Do you know how good it felt to hear, "It's all good, you have nothing to apologize for"? We may need a lot of reassurance, but with the right partner, it's not a problem. We deserve to feel safe in all our relationships.

It was time to unlearn what I deemed normal in the past and let a healthy love in, slowly but surely. I had to find a balance between being truly at peace and being able to set firm boundaries, but with the right person, boundaries are effortless and respected. They can even help you establish boundaries you didn't know you needed. You will find people with whom you can easily express your needs or concerns without your chest getting tight or your shoulders getting tense. Instead of freezing and forgetting the words, you'll find they flow. Their support will feel warm and welcoming.

I was able to slow down and choose the words that came out of my mouth and react with logic instead of emotional dysregulation. The tension in my body began to ease, and the perpetual knots in my shoulders began to unravel themselves. There was such a sense of freedom around those meant to be in my company.

The right ones exhibit that kind of love that makes you feel safe and protected. You feel comfortable enough to fall asleep in their arms. They validate your emotions and don't make you feel dumb for not knowing something. They don't scorn you when you make a mistake and, instead, hold you accountable with compassion. They remain respectful when you're fighting and do not insult you when they're angry. There's no transactional behavior or malicious intent. You're both fiercely loyal to each other and believe in and support each other's dreams. They tell jokes that make you belly-laugh and share vulnerable traumas that have shaped them into who they are today. They're gentle and tranquil, and being around them gives you a sense of peace. Your body language and aura begin to change. The glow of emotional safety is unmatched.

There's sex that makes you close your eyes and wish it was over, and there's sex that makes you open your eyes and not want it to end.

Wait for the latter. There are men who embrace the divine act of making love to a woman, and there are men who see women as nothing more than something to expel their repressed emotions into. Men, you wake up and decide every day which one you will be.

No more settling for the person who texts you, last minute, that they can't make it after you made the plans. We're picking the person who makes plans, takes us out, pays for dinner, and books a hotel on the waterfront for the weekend. We're picking the ones that brag to their friends about how smart you are and say your name in rooms filled with opportunity. We're picking someone who celebrates your wins as they would theirs. We're picking someone who you can slow-dance and play air guitar in the kitchen with. We're picking someone who enhances life so much you don't seek validation from social media. We're picking someone you can share your scar stories with, recognizing how far you've grown since you got them. Your imperfections are perfections to the right one. They'll kiss your scars and make you forget your self-doubt.

What's meant for you will never pass you by. Nothing will be too much for the one who's made for you. They will know exactly how to handle you. Together, we thrive. Together, we created a home with no tension or raised voices—a home that operates from a stance of love and compassion. It's a home I looked forward to coming back to.

I used to be a dine-and-ditcher. Now, I found someone I want to cook meals with.

Chapter 17: Kismet

I had built a very successful career in corporate—"played the game", as Mother Goose taught us. My moral compass pointed me away from the dairy team, and I climbed the corporate ladder to the point where I wanted to jump off the top of it.

So many of us are burnt out, giving away our power to our full-time jobs. Maybe it's me overcompensating for my high-functioning ADHD, but what took some people eight hours to finish, I got done in two and was forced to spend the other six asking for more work or acting busy. Maybe if we could take a siesta after lunch, as we did in college, things would be better.

Millennials entered the workforce in the worst economic crash in human history, yet we're being blamed for the economic collapse. We're in debt and depressed because we're in debt. We want to buy a house but can't afford it, yet we're wasting money paying rent. So, we're squatting with friends or are in situation-chips because you can split the rent. Anything is better than living at home (even if it's a frat house).

We are conditioned to believe that we need to slave away at a job with no meaningful impact in order to make ends meet. I had spent most of my life working toward this particular career, and before I knew it, I was burnt out and miserable. I did everything I was told to do to be successful. I took out a loan, went to college, got a full-time job, got a 401(k), bought a car, bought a house, got high-speed internet. I was "living the dream", a.k.a. wanted to die.

The world is constantly telling us the key to happiness is more. We're told to make more money so we can buy more things and drown ourselves in our false vision until we believe we're happy. Existential philosopher Albert Camus stated, "You will never be happy if you continue to search for what happiness consists of. You will never live if you are looking for the meaning of life."[1] The more money you try to make, the poorer you feel. The more friends you make, the lonelier you feel. The sexier you try to be, the less sexy you feel.

We've been thrown into a highly competitive environment, working against each other when we should be collaborating. We're drowning in work that we don't care about because it doesn't fuel our creativity. We're powerless to make a strive toward our goals because our energy is depleted due to lack of inspiration. Our high-functioning depression turned us into workaholics, so focused on trying to survive through everything that's thrown at us that we neglect our boundaries in the process. Cortisol production was supposed to be our body's way of letting us know we were in danger, and now we get it from writing emails. But we are admired as good workers, so we get more work and feel compelled to complete it.

We feel guilty about resting because we live in a society that glorifies burnout. We are basing our worth on our level of productivity and are blind to the fact that small breaks are vital. We attract bosses who mimic the trauma we experienced growing up. We feel unworthy and like we don't deserve to rest due to outside voices repeatedly telling us we're not enough and that we must do more. We

---

1. "Albert Camus Quotes." Brainy Quote. Accessed November 22, 2023. https://www.brainyquote.com/quotes/albert_camus_105605#:.

feel the need to prove ourselves and end up people-pleasing because that's the only way we gained love growing up.

So, we power through it, consuming trash caffeine, burning ourselves out. Physical ailments start to appear, and we ignore them, making them worse. We're always doing, always going, always on edge waiting for the next tragedy to occur. We don't know how to rest and relax, how to just be. Again, it takes training your brain to operate differently. Just as we trained it to be on edge, just as we can train it to practice gratitude, we can train it to release unnecessary tension. We can slowly crawl out of this dark cave and dive back into the pool of happiness.

Burnout is your soul's way of snapping you back into alignment. It's time to burn out of burnout. It's time to step back and create something we are passionate about outside of work, something exciting for ourselves that makes us fall in love with life again. But first, we must get clear on what we're passionate about. How are you going to do it if you don't know what you want? How many of us say we don't have a fun fact about ourselves because our lives now revolve around work? We're not letting life just happen to us anymore. It's time to move forward and actively create it with our thoughts and actions.

We forget life is about creating. If you're not building your own vision, you're helping someone else build theirs. By the time we're done for the day, we're too tired to do anything for ourselves—too tired to focus on our own passions, too tired to go to the gym, too tired to even cook dinner, too tired to do anything (except drink whisky or doomscroll). We're lucky if we take a shower before we crawl into bed to do it again the next day, only to grow anxious over the thought of having to do this forever.

It's hard to find a balance between working and being creative. My writing was put on the back burner for years because I was so consumed with work—work I was doing for someone else, not stimulating me intellectually or making a tangible difference in the world. I felt like I accomplished nothing.

Some of us still must "play the game" and go work our corporate jobs while things are unfolding behind the scenes. No matter where you are in life, trust that you are right where you need to be. You are always in the right place; you just have the wrong mindset. Ask yourself, "What is this trying to teach me?" rather than "Why is this happening to me?". Eventually, you'll see why you had to experience what you did. You might end up thankful in the future for what you resent in the present.

I started doing some digging to find out what R&D was up to. Their focus was on new flavors for next year and development of 100 percent recycled plastic packaging. Development takes a long time, so they continued to produce more single-use plastic packaging every day. They had no intention to halt production because they had consumers' mouths to feed. They had no plans to remediate the current damage plastic has caused for the environment, despite the backlash they were facing for being one of the world's largest plastic polluters.

Don't get me started on the plastic—plastic drove me crazy. I filled enough garbage bags full of single-use plastic tasting cups for lifetimes. I felt like I was stabbing Mother Earth in the heart. It takes a great deal of resources to make plastic, just for it to be used once and then sit in a landfill forever. All I could think about was the current pool of plastic floating in the ocean and the tons and tons of it polluting the Earth's landfills, beaches, and rivers. It's all just sitting there intact, except for the microplastics detaching from the polymer string. And I was contributing to it.

I get it; some people need products packaged with plastic due to sanitary conditions. Not everyone has access to clean food or water. But we need solutions, not Band-Aids. Instead of mass-producing plastic water bottles, why aren't we fixing the dirty water problem? Don't tell me it can't be done because we installed water filters all over Mexico City on our study abroad trip. There is no reason everyone in the world shouldn't have access to clean drinking water. There are homeless children using our dirty plastic bottles to fill up with water and hike home with it. Dirty water, and to what home? They are sleeping on filthy cots with no electricity while these corporate millionaires have multiple uninhabited homes. Some people have five houses, while others have none. Some people have private jets, and others don't have electricity. Some people are dumping tons of perfectly consumable product down the drain, and others are fishing trash out of the dumpster to find something to eat. Some have closets full of clothing that has never been worn and is gathering dust, and others don't even have shoes or a bed to sleep in at night. The world is so unbalanced. May we help restore it.

I tried to throw some ideas out there regarding environmental remediation, but no action was taken. Although change is painfully slow on a corporate level, at what point do you decide to take your energy elsewhere? Or do you keep fighting the big corporate monsters and try to make a difference from within? I fought this internal battle for years. Mother Goose had instilled the belief in us that we would truly change corporate from the inside out. So, I tried. I started out by making small changes, like replacing all the single-use petroleum-based plastic tasting cups with compostable cups made from corn. So, that was a start, but I still wasn't satisfied. I had to think bigger. I won't stop fighting until all of the plastic is out of the ocean.

I tried to pitch the idea of creating a substance to degrade plastic back into crude oil and re-enrich the Earth of its depleted nutrients, but the corporation wanted none of that. They wanted to work harder, not smarter. Saving the world was not at the top of their priority list. I knew my brain was meant for bigger things.

No inconveniences at work were as traumatic as what I endured in the past, so I was able to handle corporate chaos with ease. While working in corporate taught me how to work productively in a fast-paced environment, it instilled a false demand to be overworked most of the time. They do not leave room for rest and recovery, which is a vital part of the operation.

Working full-time is frying our brains. Work-life balance needs to make room for rest and recovery—no checking emails on Saturday or Sunday; protect your time. That will really give you the "Sunday Scaries". Why do we demonize Sunday when it's supposed to be a day for rest? Instead, we are mentally preparing for jobs we can't stand. We're leaving our loved ones and end up crying on airplanes, even in first class with vegan meals and free champagne, because all we really want is to be back in their arms and not at work.

Working in corporate taught me the discernment between intelligence and wisdom. People pride themselves on being ignorant, insulting intelligence and wisdom to make up for their lack of it. Intelligence is doing calculations to find out exactly how much citric acid you need to add to a beverage to make it a specific pH. Wisdom is knowing commercial citric acid is derived from black mold, and so those poisoned by mycotoxins from toxic mold exposure probably shouldn't be consuming whatever we're putting it into. Intelligence is knowing what to do and say in the interview to climb the corporate ladder. Wisdom is turning your hamster wheel into a staircase to climb somewhere else on your own. Wisdom comes when you start to think for yourself, when you work out your own trial and error, and question why we idolize idiots.

Science evolved from trying to understand and explain natural phenomena to creating the illusion that scientists are working to fix the problem. They now base their results on what best fits Big Pharma's narrative because Big Pharma is paying them to say so. The same people who control the poisons fed to us are the same people who control the medicine given to us when we get sick from it. The falsehood of everything is astonishing. Fake food makes fake people. Everything is so fake around us that it's almost hard to stay real.

I used my time at work wisely and became well-versed in all the chemicals, inflammatory man-made oils, and synthetic salts that are being pumped into processed food and beverages, despite not knowing the actual effect they're having on the body. Not every processed ingredient is harmful to the body, but the labeling loopholes the industry exploits make them hard to discern. Food labels are manipulated, and toxic substances are rereleased out under different names with their chemistry slightly tweaked. "Non-GMO" can still contain glyphosate. "Cage Free" doesn't mean cruelty-free—they're not in a cage but still have less than a square foot to live and are living in their own chit. "Non-Dairy" can still have milk derivatives in it. "Fat-Free" is loaded with sugar to make up for the absence of fat. "Sugar-Free" contains gut biome–destroying artificial sweeteners. "Natural Flavors" are not all natural. The list goes on.

Certain ingredients including paraffin wax, TBHQ, BHA, and food dyes leave us consuming byproducts of the petroleum industry— chemicals that are not digestible or beneficial to the human body are used as additives to preserve cheap, processed foods. Then, we are waking up the next day with acne and not able to chit. It's up to our providers to provide, and we should be able to trust them, but it's about money, power, and control, all at the expense of the consumer's health. Sick consumers make more money for Big Pharma. We are their test rats, and we are willingly volunteering by purchasing their products.

The corporate greenwashing incentives they feed you are absurd. They say "less plastic" and will give you a paper straw but in a plastic cup with a plastic lid, while continuing to produce more plastic every day. They'll give you a paper straw to save the fish, but continue industrial fishing on a commercial level. Then, the paper straw is reported to have more chemicals than single-use plastic ones. They'll pull one artificial sweetener off the shelf but release another in its place. We are being exploited by corporate and do not deserve it— neither does the Earth.

Now, I already despised the industry, but I grew to not be able to stand corporate culture. Everything about the culture became repulsive to me—working long hours to make the rich richer, increasing my salary just enough every year to make me want to stay, the false sense of urgency causing stress to everyone in the environment, the people at the top of the corporate chain who clearly did not have their chit together, the unbalance of wealth, not having a minute to have a cup of coffee and catch my breath, the pallets and pallets of my hard work thrown in the trash, wasting supplies and raw materials. Pizza parties as bribes didn't cut it for me because nowhere had vegan cheese. I found myself slurping down sugary coffees to power through the day again, eating processed foods, and repeating other harmful habits.

I would stress over the most mundane tasks. Meetings, emails, and tasting events would leave me with knots in my shoulders and my heart racing. I was gaining weight despite eating a clean diet. I couldn't fall asleep at night and when I finally did, I was grinding my teeth again. I struggled getting out of bed, and when I did, the first thing I consumed was a sugary coffee to wake up. I was so tired and wanted to be buried back in bed like during pandemic.

I came to the harsh realization that corporate didn't want to save the world, despite what they were advertising. I became aware that this was not in alignment with what I was becoming. I knew I had to do the work to move on. This happened right around the time of my Saturn Return (Coincidence? I think not).

When it's time to change, the universe will make you so uncomfortable with your current predicament that you have no choice but to change your ways. The things you were once able to tolerate repulse you now. You keep trying to pretend everything is fine, but deep down, you know it's not. Your inner voice keeps telling you that this is no longer in alignment with what you're becoming, but you're scared because where you're headed isn't in alignment with your ego.

There is healing in the presence of letting go of a certain outcome you were once attached to. Things are a certain way now, but that doesn't mean things have to be that way forever. Who would I be if I wasn't a chemical engineer with a master's degree? On paper, I'm an ideal candidate. In person, my energy will speak differently. Just goes to show you how fake you can look on paper. We're so blindly led to where we don't belong, and we stay there even if we're unhappy.

Countless people have told me, "Oh, as a chemical engineer, you'll get to travel all over the world," but what they don't tell you is that you'll only be in airports, hotel rooms, and twelve-plus-hour plant trials. They say, "You can go sightseeing and explore," but you're in the middle of nowhere, and the only attraction around you is the world's largest fork—way cool. They don't mention how much they miss (or enjoy) being away from their families or how much they can't stand their own company.

When you're not happy, do yourself a favor and don't deny it. Don't stay and try to make it work. We feel unsettled because we are here to do more. There is a better, greater plan for you. You are blocking what's meant for you if you are resisting these changes. Accept what is showing up for you with open arms. If you truly want to change and are willing to put in the work, everything else will fall into place. It involves leaving people behind who you thought were going to be in your life forever. It involves leaving jobs that are no longer aligned with who you're becoming. It requires movement.

I survived the 2022 round of corporate layoffs but now had a heavier workload with no extra pay. They fought for me to stay because they needed me, but this time I didn't feel bad. I wanted to see corporate crumble, so I took away the most valuable resource—my energy.

Once the existentialism of reality kicks in, what are you left with? Your dreams. It's scary to jump without a parachute, even scarier to not have health insurance, but it's scarier to stay somewhere you don't belong when you know it on a soul level. Starting over is better than continuing down an unfulfilling path.

After escaping from the prison of lies, the knots in my back I've had for most of my life finally undid themselves (without a massage). I knew I had made the right move. It was time to take a gamble on myself. My premier prestige was always writing a book. Writing is so important. It has the power to challenge the norms and change the narratives. History has been changed because of books. Writing gave intention to all the actions I took. Writing was there to catch me when no one else could. Writing was there to listen when I couldn't lay it upon it on anyone else's ears. No matter what life threw at me, it gave me the inspiration to write about it so I could help someone else one day. Now, I wanted to share my story. I knew I could do it, and I had an army of support behind me.

Writing a book is the hardest thing I've ever done. It's been harder than dealing with an emotionally abusive parent, harder than struggling with body dysmorphia, harder than dealing with a sister who's a drug addict, and harder than losing the loved ones closest to me. To sit with your raw, naked self staring back at you in the mirror, to observe all your pain and emotions you've tried to censor over the years, to become self-aware of your destructive habits and do the work to change course, is strenuous and emotionally taxing. Revisiting old traumas, exposing the darkness, and shining light on it to heal is demanding work, but I knew I had to do it. The solace that keeps me going is knowing that it will be part of someone else's survival guide. It's bigger than me; it's bigger than my pain and ego. It's what I've learned going through it and how I can use it to help others who are experiencing a similar situation.

Trying to be a writer with ADHD is a daunting task. I was unmotivated unless there was a time crunch; I never had an actual deadline, so I just put it off until "later". I thought to myself that I needed to go back on meds to write this book but did not want to. I started to get discouraged with myself and think: *Why can't I just write it? Why is the only time I find the motivation to write is when I'm late for something? Why do my best words come to me when I'm driving and can't write them down? Why do I need outside-influencing substances to help get the words from my head to the paper?* When I had time at home to write it, I couldn't bring myself to get up and sit down at the computer. On the rare occasion when I did, after getting coffee, eating, and putting away my phone, I sat down on the computer and opened social media instead of my manuscript. I felt like my attention was hijacked, and I was not in control.

I've written this book countless times in my head. I was always thinking of things to write. I had so many notes on my dumbphone from over the years that sitting down and organizing them was half the battle. Nothing came out as good as it sounded in my head, but it was a great start. I see why writers go on retreats and why Hunter S. Thompson did a chit ton of drugs. Getting words from the mind onto the paper is an eternal struggle.

I found some alleviation when I discovered functional nootropic mushrooms. They restore and connect neural pathways that have been damaged from past circumstances. They worked instantly and better than any ADHD medication I've tried, with no lingering destructive effects on the body, but I still couldn't get any writing done that I wanted to use. I was still living in my parents' house and so angry about everything I had been through that anything I wrote sounded like rant writing from a diary. I guess I was angrier than I thought. But by picking up a pen and writing about it, not judging the words that came out, somehow, a weight was lifted off me. It's healthier than punching holes in walls, hitting things, or yelling at people. I took time to sit with the pain rather than numbing it with substances. With every word coming out the end of the pen, I felt less and less pain.

Writing was the healthiest release for me. But now I was stuck with a bunch of rant writing and no motivation left. I was stuck in a hostile household where nobody was going to change their ways. I did what I did the last time I needed a reset—changed the scenery. I moved out of my parents' house and in with my new partner, together in our home built on a foundation of unconditional love. I found a safe space to create with no judgment.

Eventually, you think about it so much that you stop finding excuses and just sit down and fugging do it. I dedicated time every day to writing and brought my dreams to life. It fueled my creativity; it was the one hobby I did not abandon. Writing was my pathway to alignment, to do what I came here to do. The people whose help I needed with publishing, editing, and artwork showed up right on time.

I experienced much resistance to putting this out there. It's vulnerable. It's scary. What are people going to think? What am I exposing? Then, I realized it's my story and no one else's. It's my perspective. It's my experience. It was a way to bring purpose to my traumas and wounds.

I abolished my foreboding fear of failure and went for it anyway. It quelled my ego and fed my soul. Where I once experienced resistance to my authenticity, I now fiercely embrace it. There are times when you just have to believe in yourself and go for it, and it can look like leaving the life lined up in front of you to move across the country to pursue a dream.

For those brave enough to share their artwork, for those brave enough to share your personal writing out loud for others to hear, and for those who aspire to promote further inspiration, this one is for you.

You never know who you may help by telling your story. Our experiences make us who we are, and overcoming the things that tried to set us back is something to be proud of. We learn so much about ourselves by navigating these tumultuous experiences. We're recovering out loud now to give voice to those who suffered in silence before us. We're writing poetry about our scars and cherishing them, for they got us to where we are today. We're giving ourselves credit for the work we did in order to avoid becoming like those who hurt us. We're creating life rather than enduring it. We're being vulnerable and contributing our gifts to the world because nobody can bring what you can to the table.

Even if you tiptoe, make a move. Don't focus on whether you're doing enough or not; focus on the fact you're doing something. We're conditioned to always strive for more because we've been told that nothing we do is ever enough. We must abolish this way of thinking and tap back into our creativity. Once you tap into your creativity, it just flows.

Chapter 18: Save the World

L ife is one big lab experiment, and what I've concluded in this lab report is that the key to the universe is balance. But balance does not always mean a fifty-fifty split. Some things are heavier than others and require less to bring forth that balance.

We must find the balance between feeding our ego and knowing our worth. Ego says, "You have a great job, you make decent money, and you're working in the field you studied." Knowing your worth says, "I'm worth more than this, and my unique gifts and talents are being taken advantage of. I will thrive if I move elsewhere." May we align ourselves with our values and what we really want in life. The harder we try to resist, the faster we will burn out.

We must find the balance between knowing we're currently good enough to get what we desire but still striving to be better. Even though there are infinite levels of growth to unlock, we must elimi-nate the limiting beliefs we tell ourselves of how we will be worthy of something only after we've achieved something else. We are worthy now, no matter the circumstances. Our dreams are not dependent on fixing something about ourselves.

We must establish the balance between doing our research and using our discernment. There is so much false information available at our fingertips, it's scary. There are people with absolutely no credentials making videos on social media demonizing every processed ingredient on the shelf. They're fear-mongering tomato sauce and dried fruit because of necessary, harmless processing agents. Not every processed ingredient harms our health. Some are added to increase bioavailability, others are used to kill bacterial pathogens. Stressing over every processed ingredient out there will do more damage to your body than eating it will.

We must establish the balance between perseverance and patience. Even if we feel stuck, we must try to work through it while what is meant for us unfolds in divine timing. While working for what we truly want, we must continue to shine, even if we are stuck in a dark cave. Every experience we go through, good or bad, we learn from. Every person we meet is a student or a teacher, sometimes it's best to think of them as nothing more.

We must restore balance within ourselves to restore balance in the collective. No one is coming to save us. We don't need anyone to save us, so stop looking. This is a victim mentality, and we are using this as an excuse to not do anything. We must focus on what we can do, individually, to restore balance collectively. Stand up for what you believe in, even though it may mean standing alone. Speak your truth, even if there is a lump in your throat and you struggle to get the words out. Don't make an effort, make an impact.

We need all your help because we can't do this alone. We don't need everyone doing all-or-nothing, we need everyone doing something. Macro change starts with micro change, so when you personally change your daily habits, things will change on a larger scale. Don't think just because you're one person you can't make a difference. You're each a piece to a bigger puzzle, and without each piece, the puzzle can't be completed.

Daydreams balance nightmares. Go plant flowers over the places that tried to bury you. People want a revolution, but they don't want to start with themselves. When we heal ourselves, we heal the collective. Never underestimate the power of doing things on an individual level. We all share a general responsibility for humanity, or else you would not be here, as a human.

Believe it or not, you signed up to come here, at this time, to help deal with this chit chow before you incarnated into this lifetime. You picked your family, friends, and the traumas you would endure for your soul to evolve, so let's step into our power and do what we came here to do. Even if your purpose is to simply be here in the present, it's up to you to find out. I firmly believe in reincarnation, and the lessons we don't learn in this lifetime we will learn in the next, only harsher.

We must find the balance of energy to care for both the environment and the bills in our pockets. We can make money while we save the planet. I think we're past the point of trying to pretend climate change doesn't exist. It's sixty-five degrees Fahrenheit on Christmas in the northeast. Hurricanes and wildfires are running more rampant now than ever. Each year is growing to be the hottest on record. We are so focused on problems instead of solutions. Maybe we should figure out how to capitalize on saving the world, maybe then we will figure it out.

Mother Nature is out of whack because of us, and we must restore our divine balance with her. We're fighting each other over oil instead of pouring our energy into exploring alternatives. We have science at our disposal—how can we not? The advances in science and possibilities are endless.

Consumers consume and producers produce. I've been on both sides of the equation, and I can tell you we owe it to each other to work together to remediate the situation. Consumers can sit here and blame corporations for our current state, but that doesn't mean we should sit back and do nothing. We must shift our focus from placing blame to remediating the situation.

Consumers think they don't hold power on an individual level, and this is where you're wrong. Corporate is not going to do anything to change their actions because they're making too much money, but they won't keep making as much money if we don't support them. The producer produces to meet the consumer's demands. Corporations may have some control, but so do we. We have the power to consciously decide where we spend our money. We can take back our power by dictating the demand with our dollar.

We must never lose hope for a better future. The future is bright. I haven't lost faith in this harsh world; I still believe it can be saved. Scientists have cultivated mushrooms that eat plastic, the plant-based movement is gaining momentum, deforestation is decreasing, landfills are being converted into green spaces, the coral reefs are growing back, and you can now sue your state for violating your constitutional right to a clean and healthy environment by promoting fossil fuel projects and ignoring climate change. It was done in Montana, and the judge ruled in their favor. You can surrender to the fact you may not know what to do but will do what you need to do to save the Earth. Everyone's actions might look different. Never underestimate the power you hold.

It's easy to lose yourself and get sucked into the negative aspects that are present in this world. It's easier to say "everything sucks" than "life is abundant," but we must hold our high vibe. High energy always wins. (Look at yourself in the mirror and repeat that to yourself to conquer anything life throws at you.)

Your ancestors passed down more than just trauma, they also passed down generational wisdom, strength, and power. As we acknowledge and work through our generational trauma, we must also acknowledge and appreciate our generational strengths. Once you learn how to integrate everything and create your own reality, you can live an abundant life.

I am here to tell you that you can climb up from rock bottom. I went from overthinking and over-drinking to reviving and thriving. It was worth the tears, the sleepless nights, and everything I left behind when I leveled up. The real glow up is recognizing your worth and acting accordingly.

I still have more healing to do and things to work though. I still have days where I feel out of balance and my past comes back to haunt me, but I know how to handle it now. Life ebbs and flows, and nobody is thriving 100 percent of the time, but I now possess the self-awareness to notice when I am not thriving and can take the steps to get back there.

I didn't know where to end this—more life kept happening that I wanted to include. My book got published, my sister got her chit together, I moved to paradise with my new phamily, and started a new, fun, fulfilling project that made me money on my own time. (There are so many other ways to make money rather than working for corporate. I could write a separate book on the energy of money alone.) But above all, I finally feel like I am doing enough.

Even after publishing an autobiography, I feel as if life is just beginning. Stay tuned for my next book to see where life takes me. I've been working on this one for almost a decade, and if I don't end this chit now, I'll be stumbling around like Bilbo Baggins at the end of my life, looking for somewhere quiet to sit and finish my book. The time has come to get this message out for those who need it now.

I wish you all the best along your journey. I leave you with these words. You are stronger than you know. You can do it. Now, go be monumental.

- May we dig deep, shine light in the dark places, and find the devotion and desire to get better.
- May we pull up our pain by its roots and bring it to the surface to alchemize.
- May we assemble the patience to work through our pain and move forward without inflicting it on others.
- May we establish healthy boundaries so we can receive what we truly need.
- May we take intentional action to follow our passions and create.
- May we repair, upgrade, uplift, restore, and bring out the best in each other.

- May we remain humble, divinely guided, and divinely protected.
- May we stand firm in our truths but remain teachable and normalize changing our thoughts based on new information.
- May we shift to collaboration instead of competition, creation instead of consumption.
- May we recognize the difference between what's no longer serving us and what's worth fighting for.
- May we fight for it and thrive in life.

Acknowledgments

I would like to extend my deepest gratitude to all of those who have assisted me on my journey—both those who taught me the harshest lessons and those who were there to hold my hand as I lifted myself back up. I would like to thank those who have shown their unconditional support as I navigated my inner turmoil. This book would not be possible without you.

Thank you to those who have inspired me to do better and have held me accountable with compassion.

Thank you to those who have encouraged me to pursue my dreams and have provided me a safe space to do so.

Thank you to those who have influenced me to explore my creative side. Life would have been dull and boring without you.

I am grateful for all that has been given and for all that has been taken away, for the closed doors, detours, and roadblocks protecting me from the paths not meant for me.

I am grateful to the universe for lining up everything I needed to get where I was going.

I am grateful for yesterday, today, and the days yet to come.

I am grateful to each and every one of you for reading this.

Thank you,
—Claire

Glossary

ADHD: Attention-deficit hyperactivity disorder

BHA: Butylated Hydroxyanisole

BEC: Bacon, egg & cheese

BECSPK: Bacon, egg & cheese, salt, pepper, ketchup

ChemE: Chemical engineer. Pronounced "chem-ie"

Chit: Shit but with a "ch." See chapter 6 for the background story

Chine: Shine but with a "ch"

Choes: Shoes with a "ch"

Chot: Shot with a "ch"

Chower: Shower with a "ch"

CPTSD: Complex post-traumatic stress disorder

Dumbphones: Smartphones that are actually dumbing us down

Fug: Less vulgar version of fuck

GMO: Genetically modified organism

HFCS: High-fructose corn syrup

Phamily: My soul family I met through listening to the band Phish

STEM: Science, technology, engineering, and mathematics

Glossary

TBHQ: tert-Butylhydroquinone
Thurfraturday: Thursday to Sunday

www.ingramcontent.com/pod-product-compliance
Lightning Source LLC
Chambersburg PA
CBHW070659130626
46553CB00005B/1771